Come Back Moo

Come Back Moo

The Story of a Good Man

A Memoir by William B. Mead

**The New
Atlantian Library**

The New Atlantian Library
is an imprint of
ABSOLUTELY AMAZING eBOOKS

Published by Whiz Bang LLC, 926 Truman Avenue, Key West, Florida 33040, USA

Come Back Moo copyright © 2013, 2014 by William B. Mead. Electronic compilation / print editions copyright © 2013, 2014 by Whiz Bang LLC.

All rights reserved. No part of this book may be reproduced, scanned, or transmitted in any form or by any means, electronic or mechanical, including photocopying, recording, or any information storage and retrieval system, without permission in writing from the publisher. Please do not participate in or encourage piracy of copyrighted materials in violation of the author's rights. Purchase only authorized ebook editions.

This work is based on factual events. While the author has made every effort to provide accurate information at the time of publication, neither the publisher nor the author assumes any responsibility for errors, or for changes that occur after publication. Further, the publisher does not have any control over and does not assume any responsibility for author or third-party websites or their contents.

For information contact:
Publisher@AbsolutelyAmazingEbooks.com

ISBN-13: 978-0692332627
ISBN-10: 0692332626

Other books by William B. Mead

American Averages: Amazing Facts of Everyday Life
(with Mike Feinsilber)
Baseball, the Presidents' Game (with Paul Dickson)
Even the Browns: Baseball During World War II
Two Spectacular Seasons
The Official New York Yankees Hater's Handbook
Low and Outside: Baseball in the 1930's
The Explosive Sixties
The Inside Game

Acknowledgements

For decades, my brother and I have taken turns as custodian of a very thick and very old loose-leaf notebook which we call, simply, "The Bowmar Book." The first reference is to a Bowmar ancestor arriving from England in 1635. The pages are neatly preserved in plastic covers. Most are typewritten. All are literate. It is a heckuva read, taking a frontier family from Virginia to Kentucky, through battles against Indians and—this being a Southern family—Union soldiers, and on through Twentieth Century life.

The Bowmar Book provided the foundation for my search into the life and times of Herman Bowmar, a man of immense goodness, achievement and joy who was my grandfather. His ninety-two years provide a clear window on the striving and (largely) virtuous America of the Twentieth Century.

As I worked, family members pitched in. Alden Mead, my brother, shared memories and advice. Tom van der Voort, my cousin, and—especially—his wife, Elizabeth, fleshed out the Bowmar family heritage in Versailles, Kentucky, where Tom's grandfather, Aitchison Alexander Bowmar, edited the weekly newspaper and wrote much of The Bowmar Book.

Come Back Moo

("Uncle Aitchee" was my grandfather's eldest brother). Marti Martin of the Woodford County (Kentucky) Historical Society dug up wonderful clippings and other background material on life in Versailles, and her colleague Dona Wilson fleshed out the Bowmar family tree and explained laws and attitudes about intra-family marriages.

Perhaps the most dramatic episode in my grandfather's life concerned his late-in-life marriage to Paula Aulik, a heroic refugee from war-torn Estonia who somehow got herself and her five children through the horrors of Soviet and Nazi cruelty and, finally, to the United States. Her children Helju, Arvo and Jaak told me their story in dramatic detail and provided photos.

I thank Paul Dickson, author of more than sixty books, for advice and photos; Jack Limpert, distinguished editor of The Washingtonian magazine for more than forty years, for encouragement and advice; Mike Feinsilber, my old newspapering colleague, for the same; our son, Chris Mead, and his son, Kevin Mead—our eldest grandchild—for family insights and editorial encouragement; Brett Mead, our second grandson, for surprising historical documents about the Bowmar family; Richard Bright on slot machines; David and Barbara Kaldahl and their daughter, Beth Kaldahl Schupp, on Fair Hills Resort; John C. Danforth, the former U.S. senator, on his grandfather, William C. Danforth. Particular thanks to Marc Nathan, the world's most skilled and patient guide to computer mysteries.

These are my friends. Jenny Mead, my wife of fifty-seven years, encouraged me and, as always, contributed to my pleasant life. So did our sons, Chris and Andy, and Chris's wife and their three sons.

Also:

Primm, James Neal. *Lion of the Valley: St. Louis, Missouri, 1764-1980*. Missouri Historical Society Press, 1981.

Philpott, Gordon M. *Daring Venture: The Life Story of William H. Danforth*. Random House, 1960.

Vexler, Robert I. *St. Louis; A Chronological and Documentary History, 1762-1970*. Oceana Publications Inc., 1974.

Courtaway, Robbi. *Wetter Than the Mississippi: Prohibition in Saint Louis and Beyond*. Reedy Press, 2008.

Culver, John C. and Hydge, John. *American Dreamer: The Life and Times of Henry A. Wallace*, W.W. Norton, 2002.

Fey, Marshall. *Slot Machines: An Illustrated History of America's Most Popular Coin-Operated Gaming Device*. Stanley Paher, Nevada Publications, 1983.

Mead. Chris. *Champion: Joe Louis, Black hero in White America*, Charles Scribner's Sons, 1985.

Ottenheimer, Martin. *Forbidden Relatives: The American Myth of Cousin Marriage.* University of Illinois, 1996.

Come Back Moo

The Story of a Good Man

Moo read to us every night, after dinner. He read Mark Twain's *Tom Sawyer* and *Huckleberry Finn*, Rudyard Kipling's *Jungle Book* and *Ricki-Ticki Tavi*, tales of King Arthur and the Knights of the Roundtable, Ernest Thompson Seaton's *Wild Animals I Have Known*, Joel Chandler Harris's *Uncle Remus*.

Moo read with joy. He was Uncle Remus, with dialect he learned growing up in rural Kentucky. He read exciting passages with excitement. We were lucky little boys, my brother Alden, and I, though we didn't know it.

Moo was our grandfather. His real name was Herman Bowmar. Maw was our grandmother. Her real name was Fanny Bowmar, though she considered "Fanny" undignified, and went by Frances. When Alden was a toddler, he started calling them Moo and Maw. I came along sixteen months after Alden.

Moo was general manager of the cereal department at Ralston Purina. Hot Ralston, in the 1930's and '40's, was a mainstream breakfast cereal. Wheat Chex—then called Shredded Ralston—was gaining popularity among cold cereals. Ry Krisp was a popular cracker, and Ralston made oatmeal under store brands such as A&P and Kroger. The family was prosperous, even during the Depression.

William B. Mead

More important to Alden and me, Ralston sponsored the adventures of Tom Mix, a good-guy, shoot-em-up cowboy, on the radio every evening at 5 or 5:30. (Television didn't come along until after World War II.) Moo would try to get home from the office in time to listen with us. He would lie on his back and clear his nasal passages by squeezing a bulb and shooting some forgotten substance up his nose.

Tom Mix

You don't know Tom Mix? He was the original cowboy movie hero and he was the real thing—a former rodeo champ. He made 336 movies (336!) between 1910 and 1935, most of them silent, and at his peak Fox paid him $7,500 a week. A three-year circus gig paid him even more-- $20,000 a week. He got young John Wayne his first movie job, loading props for Fox. Mix was a pallbearer at Wyatt Earp's funeral in 1929, and he cried.

Mix was one of fifty horsemen who rode in Teddy Roosevelt's inaugural parade in 1909. He wasn't famous then but he was very famous in 1933 when he rode his horse Tony down Pennsylvania Avenue as a star of FDRs inaugural parade. A very important man, with a fair number of Hollywood wives(5).

He did his own riding stunts so he occasionally got busted up. He died in 1940 when he slammed on the brakes in his nifty 1937 Cord 812 Phaeton and a metal briefcase, on a shelf just behind his head, whammed forward and broke his neck. The case was heavy with cash and jewels.

Tom Mix, in action.

Moo and Maw were first cousins. Maw was born in 1880, Moo in 1881. They grew up in Versailles, Kentucky, the county seat of Woodford County. *(That's Ver-SALES, USA, not Vair-sigh'. The Vairsigh version of Versailles is in France. My father's family, the Meads, farmed outside Greenwich, Ohio. That's GREEN-wich, USA, not Grennage, England.*

The Bowmar cousins wed September ninth, 1903, at the home of the bride's mother, on High Street in Versailles. The bride wore white organdy, trimmed with lace, and carried a bouquet of Bride roses. "Woodford never gave up a sweeter daughter than the bride of yesterday," proclaimed *The Woodford Sun*, "nor ever sent out a truer son than the young fellow to whom she has plighted her troth." The *Sun* was owned and edited by the young fellow's older brothers, Aitchee and Dan Bowmar.

Maw's maiden name was Bowmar, so after marriage she was Fanny Bowmar Bowmar, though she always signed herself as Frances B. Bowmar. As cousins, they thought they should not reproduce. The conventional wisdom held that children born to first cousins were likely to be handicapped, as indicated in this verse from slavery times.

> *Sally's in de garden siftin' sand.*
> *And all she want is a honey man.*
> *De reason why I wouldn't marry,*
> *Because she was my cousin*
> *O, row de boat ashore, hey, hey*
> *Sally's in de garden siftin sand.*

Even so, cousin marriages were not controversial or unusual, and had often been encouraged as a way to keep land and money in the family. Dona Wilson has compiled hundreds of family trees for the Woodford County Historical Society, and came across many cousin marriages. Until 1893, just ten years before Moo and Maw married, Kentuckians could legally marry their brothers, sisters, aunts, uncles, and grandparents, although Ms. Wilson found few, if any, such unions. Kentucky didn't outlaw first cousin marriages until 1942. Many modern scientists dismiss the theory of handicapped offspring as a myth. Nineteen states and all European countries permit marriage between first cousins.

Moo and Maw surely used contraception , but they wanted children, and tragedy brought them one. Maw's older sister, Charlotte Sessions, died in childbirth. The baby's father wasn't in position to raise a baby—"he drank," we were darkly told, when the painful subject finally was explained in our adolescence—so Moo and Maw eagerly took in the baby and named her Charlotte. That was in 1905, although the formal adoption wasn't registered for more than a decade.

William B. Mead

Charlotte was our mother. Our father was Chester Alden Mead, whom mother met at Oberlin College, in Ohio. Back then Oberlin was very conservative when it came to relationships—no, we better just call them friendships—between male and female students. It was out in the country, far from the seductive pleasures of city life. Just right, Moo thought, for his pretty and sociable daughter. Oberlin was so strict that Moo, while in Ohio on business, had to get special permission to take his daughter and her roommate to dinner.

Come Back Moo

Mother (second from left) with cousins and friends on the Fishback farm outside Versailles, Kentucky, in 1927. She was twenty-two and would marry three years later.

Mother came from the silver-spoon background provided by Moo and Maw. Our father grew up on a small farm. When Alden and I visited his parents in the 1940's, their farmhouse still lacked running water and telephone service; electricity had just reached them, courtesy of the New Deal's Rural Electrification Administration. They proudly made a living on 100 acres, raising a son and a daughter, not to mention chickens, turkeys, hogs, sheep, milk cows, two plow horses and a border collie named Shep.

Our father earned a scholarship to Oberlin, which was nearby, and waited tables in the women's dining room. That's where he met Mother. They held hands under a blanket at college football games, fell in love, graduated together, and married two years later, in 1930, after our father paid off his college debts

He had planned to teach school, but Moo convinced him that he'd make a better living selling animal feeds for Ralston Purina, the company for which Moo worked. That was the backbone of the business—Purina Chows, sold to farmers to feed their livestock. They were stationed in the Midwestern farm- belt town of Jackson, Ohio. Mother loved the small-town life. With a friendly approach and his farm background, our father sold a lot of Chows.

Until the Great Depression struck, hitting farmers hard. As farm income declined 64 percent in the 1930's, sales of Purina Chows tanked. Ralston Purina laid off half its salesmen. Then they laid off half of those who were left. Our father survived the first cut, but not the second. So the young couple moved in with Moo and Maw— Mother's parents. Their home was a big, white, comfortable house in Webster Groves, Missouri, a green and pleasant suburb of St. Louis. Moo and Maw had moved there from the city so Maw, sick with tuberculosis, could breathe the clean country air. It worked; she fully recovered. (St. Louis was notoriously smoky and dark, worse than Pittsburgh by some measures, because industry and homes burned soft coal mined in nearby Southern Illinois. From the *St. Louis Post-Dispatch*, December 23, 1926: "Presumably the sun rose, but whether it did nobody knows.")

Come Back Moo

Maw, in the kind of formal portrait that was fashionable before camera technology made snapshots popular. About 1940, in the Bowmar living room in Webster Groves, Missouri.

William B. Mead

The young couple's move was to be temporary, of course, until our father-to-be found a job. Alden was born December 9, 1932, and I followed April 1, 1934. Our father did what many desperate young men did during the Depression. Through a friend of Moo's, he got a job selling life insurance. It paid no salary—just commissions. "Business isn't so hot but not so bad, either," he wrote to his parents on June 5 of 1934. "My income has been: April about $75, May $85 and already in June $90 so you see things look better." A month later he was dead, felled by a strep germ that today would be quickly cured with antibiotics.

Mother grieved deeply, for years. I remember her crying at the dinner table. Trying to comfort her, Maw said, "Yes, Charlotte, but you have the boys, and us." "I know," Mother sobbed, "but I want Chet!" Chet's death killed her faith in an all-powerful and loving god.

Hard as it was for Mother, the loss was a mild one for Alden and me. Alden was twenty months old and I was an infant. Alden remembered our father only faintly, and I not at all. Moo and Maw made us feel wanted, even prized. Moo eagerly assumed the role of father, resigning his country club membership so he could spend weekends with his grandsons rather than with his golf buddies.

Our father's death made our living arrangement permanent. Moo and Maw expanded the house, moving into a new master bedroom and bath. They added a playroom and half-bath downstairs for Alden and me, and had a swing set installed in the back yard. It was set in concrete; no flimsy swings for their grandsons!

William B. Mead

Maw and Moo with grandson Alden, 1933.

Maw taught school before marrying but stayed home thereafter, in line with custom. Mother, a young widow, stayed home to care for Alden and me, but once we started school she wanted to work. Moo was opposed. A Southern gentleman, he believed, took care of his women. He told Mother he would stop her allowance if she broke tradition.

She did, walking to work every morning at the Webster Trust Company. She needed the outlet and the bank profited from her friendly personality and widespread local friendships. She sacrificed the allowance and the issue subsided.

Maw's life was soft but structured. She endured a facial tic – the right side of her face twitched continuously. Her kindness and patience influenced all of us. Her social life was built around our neighborhood and The First Congregational Church of Webster Groves, as was Mother's.

The Bowmar household ran on a strict schedule, set by Moo. Dinner was at 6pm, precisely. Life was more formal back then, and Moo would appear at the table wearing a smoking jacket (he didn't smoke), a casually decorative garment cut like a sport coat. He said grace. We had maids – "colored women," in the vernacular of the day. This was in line with Moo's and Maw's Kentucky background, and indeed with much of America. Having a maid in the 1930's and '40's was the social and economic equivalent today of shopping at Whole Foods, drinking latte at Starbucks, and dining out or getting carryout two or three times a week.

Moo and Maw were such fair and generous employers that from my early childhood until their deaths in their nineties, they employed only three maids. Effie, whom Alden and I called MyMy, took sick and died when I was perhaps seven years old. Vernice Mitchell, a tall, cheerful woman with a big laugh, retired in her sixties. Ruth Sleet, perhaps the best cook in the world, prepared three meals a day for Moo and Maw the rest of their lives.

We ate well. At table, Maw summoned the maid by either tinkling a little bell or stepping on a pedal, installed under the rug, that buzzed in the kitchen. *More biscuits please, Ruth. Yes ma'am.* We ate freshly baked hot bread every evening on a three-night cycle—biscuits, corn muffins, parker house rolls. Alden and I ate vegetables under duress, and Moo carved, expertly. No one could carve a turkey as well as Moo.

Maw preferred the dark meat. She also drank hot tea, with lemon, at lunch, ate whole wheat bread in a white bread era, and drank skim milk. Milk was delivered in glass bottles, with a bulb at the top. The milk wasn't homogenized, so the cream rose into that bulb. To get whole milk, you shook it all up. To get skim milk, you poured off the cream, put it in a jar or pitcher, and used it for your coffee or cereal. We poured it on our hot Ralston, a breakfast staple in the Bowmar house. Leftover Ralston was formed into patties and fried for lunch. Cream of Wheat was banned because it competed with Ralston. For the same reason, Alden and I were discouraged from listening to *Jack Armstrong, the All-American Boy*, a popular radio show sponsored by Wheaties.

After reading to Alden and me in the evening, Moo put us to bed. He was jolly. When Moo and Maw went to bed at 10pm sharp Moo would look in on us to make sure we were covered and comfortable.

Moo, grandfather in father role, took Alden and me for walks on Sunday afternoons to see "the buildings" – a row of nearby houses under construction. He took us to the first game of the 1942 World Series and the last game of the '43 Series (The hometown Cardinals lost both games. They beat the Yankees in the '42 series but lost to the same team in '43).

Stan Musial. *He was a rookie when we saw him help the Cardinals beat the Yankees in the 1942 World Series.*

Moo took us to two performances of Blackstone the Magician, who sawed a woman in half and levitated a woman, defying gravity. He took us to Barnum & Bailey's circuses and to Buffalo Bill's Wild West Show. (Buffalo Bill Cody died in 1917, but his show lived on.) As we got older, Moo and Maw took us to traveling performances of Broadway hit shows, including Rogers and Hammerstein's *South Pacific*.

Moo was a man of habit. He took a cold shower every morning, washed his hair, and wore a hat at breakfast to keep his hair in place. This was downright eccentric, since few people bathed more than once or twice a week. He shaved with an electric razor—a newfangled gadget—and was ahead of the curve in other ways. Most families heated their houses with coal, delivered in the winter by the same truck that brought ice in the summer to keep food cool. That truck didn't stop at the Bowmar house, which was heated by natural gas and boasted an electric refrigerator in the kitchen. It also featured three full bathrooms upstairs—most families had one—plus the half-bath downstairs.

Soon after Oldsmobile introduced the first automatic transmission in 1939, the Bowmar garage featured two big black Olds sedans with HydraMatic drive. When those cars shifted from first gear to second and then to third, you could feel the change, and hear it. Every Saturday morning Alden and I would pile in with Moo as he drove to Dodge and Bollmeir to fill the tank and have the oil checked and the windshield washed. Self-service filling stations were far in the future, and when they did come along Moo and Maw stuck to full-service pumps. Moo listened to the news on the radio on his way to and from work. After retiring in 1945, he stopped buying cars with radios.

Moo's schedule governed the details of family life, and Mother used to tease him about it. He never wavered. On family vacations, he and Maw ate an early breakfast and were on the first tee at 8:30, Moo golfing and Maw picking up discarded tees. He delighted in companionship, particularly from Alden and me, but if we didn't show up until, say, 8:45, we'd find him putting on the second green.

After Moo died in 1973, at age ninety-two, I found in his papers fifteen two-inch by three-and-a-half inch pocket diaries, each covering a year—1913 plus various years from 1936 to 1971. Diaries for other years were lost, and Moo never mentioned that he kept diaries. They included Moo's Ten Commandments, self-authored entirely to guide his own life. They were repeated, in several diaries.

1. Thou shalt purge thyself of all prejudices.
a. Religious
b. Economic
c. Nationalistic
d. Racial
2. Thou shalt learn to recognize and resist propaganda.
a. Repetition
b. Over-simplification
c. Appeal to prejudice
d. Distortion of fact
e. Coercion

3. Thou shalt eschew all expediency.

4. Thou shalt recognize and resist all rationalization.

5. Thou shalt seek all possible points of view.

6. Thou shalt learn to endure the agony of suspended judgment.

7. Thou shalt act in terms of the evidence of preponderance of probability.

8. Thou shalt define ambiguities and controversial terms.

9. Thou shalt avail thyself of the efficacy of faith.

10. Thou shalt learn to lose oneself in love.

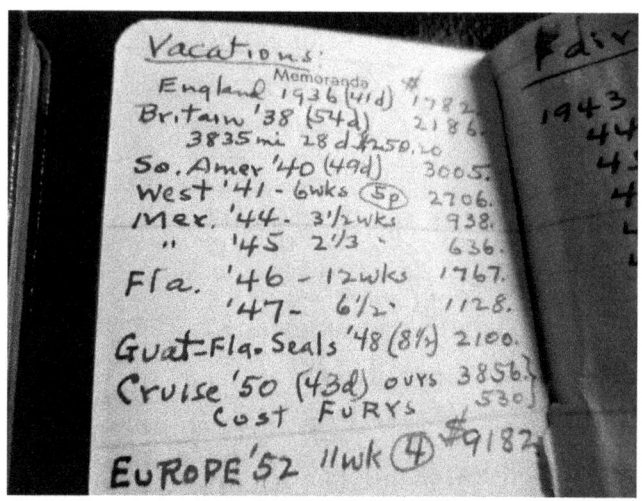

Moo never mentioned these rules, never proselytized. He also included virtuous statements by others.

"It is worth a thousand pounds a year to have the habit of looking on the bright side of things— Dr. Samuel Johnson."

Honesty: "The entire absence and complete freedom from any intent to deceit (sic) or fraud."

"To be what we are and to become what we are capable of becoming is the only end of life. – Robert Louis Stevenson."

From the diaries, we know that Moo stood five feet eight and one-half inches and weighed 154 pounds. His complexion was ruddy and his hair and eyes were gray. His hat size was seven and one-eighth, his gloves were seven Cadet and his VanReed collars were size fifteen and one-half. His socks were size ten (when did one-size-fits-all socks come along?) and his shoes were businessman's black oxfords, size seven and one-half A-AAA. He shined them himself

The diaries were not short on detail. As of January 15, 1947, the right rear tire on Moo's 1942 Oldsmobile, having been regularly rotated, had logged 4,466 miles as a right front tire, 3,106—and counting—as right rear, 3,194 as left front, and 5,145 as left rear. That car cost $1,562.64 [$17,681 in 2010 dollars] less $612.64 for trading in the 1939 Olds. The price included tax of $30.64.

Moo didn't talk much about himself, and his diaries are impersonal, with little mention of Maw, Mother, Alden or me. His life and his habits exemplified a man of self-confidence, self-made and secure in his own choices. A model of eccentric independence, Moo must have been one of the last men to wear collarless white shirts with separate collars, not to mention one-piece underwear combining boxer shorts with undershirt. Local stores no longer carried these items; Moo had to order them by mail. The diaries didn't point this out, but it is family lore.

Moo wore rimless bifocals and conservative suits made by J.W. Losse, an uppercrust St. Louis tailor. He had his hair cut at the downtown Missouri Athletic Club (MAC), where he ate lunch almost every business day. His luncheon companions were not from Ralston Purina but from other leading businesses and law firms. Most of them were Republicans, and Moo loved arguing with them. His political leanings gradually moved toward the left, influenced by his voluminous reading and by Pulitzer's liberal *St. Louis Post-Dispatch*. Moo called himself an independent, but he voted for Franklin Roosevelt three times, straying only to support Wendell Wilkie in the 1940 presidential election. In 1948 he voted for Democrat Harry Truman although the *Post-Dispatch* wrinkled its nose at Truman because of his fidelity to the Prendergast political machine of Kansas City.

Moo was a friendly man. He did not put on airs, and people liked him. Yet he carried himself with such dignity that almost everyone called him "Mr. Bowmar." After retiring in 1945, he began wearing sport shirts with his suit trousers and black shoes. That was a big move, but not as big as when his wife and daughter persuaded him to buy a car that wasn't black. It was dark green. An Oldsmobile, of course. Moo thought Cadillac drivers were showing off. Imported cars were not yet on the American scene.

Moo's dignity did not keep him from expressing love. During an auto trip when Alden and I were perhaps ten and twelve, we could tell that Moo and Maw were nervous. They pulled to the side of the road. Boys, Moo said, it's time you learned a family secret. Your Mother is not really our daughter. She is Maw's niece, whose mother died in childbirth. So we are not your blood grandparents. Please, do not love us any less...*How could we?*

We took their love for granted. Perhaps all children do. I never stopped to think how extraordinarily lucky we were, fatherless children supported and embraced by loving grandparents. When I went off to college in 1951, Mother reminded me of our good fortune and often pressed me to write letters to Moo and Maw. I considered her reminders a nuisance. I am shamed by this memory. (Letters, sealed, stamped, and mailed, were the standard means of communication. The internet was decades in the future. Long-distance phone calls were so expensive they were used only for emergencies.)

Moo didn't drink, and didn't approve of drink. St. Louis, with its large German population, boasted lots of breweries. Stag, Hyde Park, Falstaff, Griesedieck Brothers (really!), and Alpen Brau were local brewers—not the premium craft brewers of today, but beers priced low enough to undercut Budweiser in its home market.

(The Griesediecks were a large brewing family; Stag and Falstaff were also owned by Griesediecks.) Through downtown business connections, Moo was given two or three cases of beer every Christmas. "Foul stuff!" he would sneer, and give it away. One holiday season I watched him patiently uncap beer after beer—twenty-four in a case—and pour it all down the kitchen sink. During World War II Moo and Maw signed up to host soldiers for Sunday dinner. The polite young men who arrived at the Bowmar house were fed a wonderful meal, with milk, tea or coffee. I don't recall requests for stronger beverages, but a young soldier on his only day off might have wept inside.

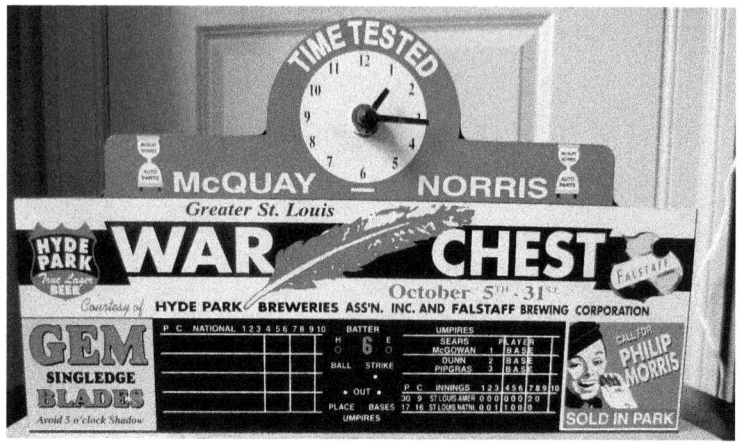

Scoreboard at Sportsman's Park, home of the St. Louis Cardinals and Browns until 1966. Note ads for Hyde Park and Falstaff, two of the five local beers that competed with Budweiser.

"I'm afraid I would like it too much," Moo said, explaining his abstinence. He had reason. His paternal grandfather and his father were alcoholics, though he never said so. His father, Daniel Mayes Bowmar Jr., is almost beatified in family journals, but he was almost surely mentally ill as well, and he died under grisly circumstances that strongly indicate suicide.

Daniel Bowmar moved from Versailles, Kentucky, to Chicago in 1865, at age twenty-two, leaving the defeated and impoverished Confederacy in pursuit of the Yankee dollar. He worked for a fire insurance company, did well, and borrowed money to buy its stock, eventually owning the company. He could not have chosen a more untimely business.

> *Late one night when we were all in bed*
> *Old Mother Leary left a lantern in the shed*
> *And when the cow kicked it over*
> *She winked her eye and said*
> *There'll be a HOT time in the old town tonight.*
> *FIRE! FIRE! FIRE!*

Whether Mother Leary was responsible or not, the great Chicago fire of 1871 killed hundreds of people, destroyed four square miles of the city, and bankrupted Daniel Bowmar's Mutual Security Insurance Company.

Meantime he had married, choosing a woman of Kentucky heritage, and fathered three children, with five more to come, including Moo. From the *Chicago Inter Ocean* in 1874: (The *Inter Ocean* newspaper was published from 1865 until 1914.)

"Our readers will be pained to hear that Daniel M. Bowmar, the popular and able insurance agent of the firm of Bowmar & Waller, 164 and 166 LaSalle street, was yesterday found to be insane by a jury impaneled before Judge Farwell to try the question of insanity. It is understood that the malady first discovered itself after the trouble consequent on the great fire of October 1871. It broke out again with great violence a few days since, and Mr. Bowmar was obliged to be confined in a straight jacket and manacled at the ankles to prevent his doing mischief. The chief features of the disease as developed, are a desire to take human life, which renders it dangerous for him to be at large. He was taken last night to the Insane Asylum, at Elgin. It is supposed that the intense mental work has led to this sad occurrence, which is a warning to businessmen of this city to abstain from overwork. The friends of Mr. Bowmar will have the sympathy of the public in their lamentable affliction."

He somehow recovered, supported his young family, revived the company, paid off its claims and debts and accumulated some wealth. He was truly a man of accomplishment.

But he suffered "a breakdown in health," as his oldest son, Aitcheson Alexander Bowmar, wrote. He sold the company, moved with his family back to Versailles, bought a share of the county's weekly newspaper, ran it for a year and a half, and then, feeling better, returned to Chicago and re-entered the insurance business. "Its (Chicago's) business maelstrom had whirled him around and cast him ashore, but its far off roar ever lingered in his ear," explained the newspaper.

The cycle repeated—successful Chicago insurance business interrupted by another breakdown in health, another return to Versailles, another purchase of *The Woodford Sun*. He couldn't keep it up, and in 1885 turned over the weekly, barely profitable, to his oldest sons, Aitcheson (Aitchie), eighteen, and Dan Jr., sixteen. By then Herman Bowmar—Moo—was four. Aitchee wrote of their father: "His life was divided between determined efforts to go forward and serious illnesses which stopped everything." Aitchee was a brilliant writer and editor, his memory still revered in Versailles. He wrote much family history, always in terms so glowing and archaic as to tickle a modern reader. Example:

"One of the most striking characteristics of the Bowmar men is their selection, generation after generation, of the highest types of wives, women of strength and character, of refinement, of purity, of fine minds, of spirituality, of competence, of social ease and charm, of wisdom, women who regard the making of homes, the rearing of children wisely and oneness with their husbands, as being among life's most priceless opportunities." (One sentence, 69 words. Continue) "There is no question in my mind that these grand women in our family have had far more to do with the high level maintained through the years, in regard to the most precious values, than we Bowmar men have."

So Aitchee, in his voluminous and glowing writings of family history, was not about to identify his father's illnesses as mental or alcoholic, both of which were considered moral weaknesses. But he came clean in a 1906 letter to the Northwestern Mutual Life Insurance Company.

Moo's oldest brother Aitchee, the country editor and family scribe.

In appealing the firm's rejection of his application for a policy, Aitchee recited the fine health and long accomplished lives of ancestors ("My great grandfather Bowmar was a noted Indian fighter..") and, to be fair, the few exceptions: "My grandfather, Herman Bowmar Jr., died at 58, of dropsy of the heart, induced by the use of liquor. (He was also a prominent orator and comic entertainer)...In all the history of the Bowmar family I have failed to find any case of insanity but my father's..." And this about his mother, and Moo's: "She was a frightful sufferer from constipation for many years before her death, and was also, though not at all a large eater, an extremely imprudent one."

In a brief autobiographical sketch, Daniel Bowmar (Moo's father) talked of living the life of a young and impoverished preacher, wearing hand-me-down clothes, before quitting the clergy because of "deficient qualification and a lack of vital piety." Besides, he was broke and in debt. He was bailed out by an older friend who said: "Take it, and as you prosper, help every young man in his need, especially when you think as well of him as I do of you." Moo took that to heart a generation later, and that family tradition of joyful generosity led to an exceptional romance in his last years.

Moo's father obviously pulled himself up, attaining wealth and respect both in the Chicago insurance business and in Kentucky journalism circles. His oldest sons, Aitchee and Dan, had been running *The Woodford Sun* for five years when this headline appeared in the January 2, 1890, edition of the *Chicago Daily Tribune*:

WAS IT MURDER?
Daniel M. Bowmar's Mutilated
Remains Found in Indiana
THROWN OR FELL OFF A CAR
His Pocketbook Found Empty,
But No Other Trace of Foul Play
ON HIS WAY TO VISIT FRIENDS
Formerly a Newspaper Publisher at Woodford,
  Kentucky
WELL KNOWN IN CHICAGO CIRCLES

Moo's father, the father of eight beginning with Aitchee and Dan Jr., had purchased a train ticket on the sleeper from Chicago to Louisville. About four am he apparently rose from his berth; dressed, from hat to boots; walked to the back of the train; and plunged off, to his death. He was forty-seven. The train was between stations. His body was cut to pieces by the next train. Moo was fatherless at nine, and his mother, suffering from heart illness and other maladies, couldn't care for him. His brother Dan Jr., who was twelve years older, married in 1892 and took in Moo, who wrote this little-boy letter to his grownup brother as Dan Jr. and bride were honeymooning:

> "Dear Dan;
> I am so glad that you and Sister (Dan's bride, Cicely de Graffenreid McCaw Bowmar) are so happy. You have gotten five presents since you left. Mr. Browning sent a pickle stand, Miss Margaret Thornton sent a beautiful brass lamp with a yellow globe, Mrs. Lyle and Rosebud sent silver and Miss Harrison sent a vase of flowers. I was playing with some dogs yesterday when one run (sic) up against me and knocked me down on the pavement, and hurt my right shoulder. I can't write any more now because my shoulder hurts me.
> With many kisses for you and Sister, I am
> Your loving brother
> Herman"

Moo finished eighth grade, then had to quit school and go to work. He was thirteen. His ailing mother suffered a fatal stroke ("apoplexy") six years later. *The Woodford Sun* couldn't support another young Bowmar; Aitchee and Dan moonlighted to make ends meet. Moo looked to railroads, the growing, romantic industry of the time. The U.S had lots of railroads back then, and Moo clerked for at least three of them, starting in Versailles and moving north. From the January 20, 1903 edition of the *Louisville Times*:

**FINE BERTH
FOR A FINE BOY**
Herman Bowmar, of Versailles Goes
With the Chicago Great Western Railway

The new job was in St. Paul, Minnesota. "Mr. Bowmar is only twenty-one years old," the story continued, "and is a young man of great promise."

Moo and Maw married in Versailles that September (1903) and moved into a St. Paul boarding house, where they lived for six months before finding "a cozy flat," as described by the always-approving *Woodford Sun*.

The young Bowmars were on their own, though bolstered by an unusual array of ancestors deeply involved in the events and traditions of their times and place. They fought Indians, owned slaves and fought for the Confederacy in the Civil War.

ROBERT BOWMAR, Moo's great-great grandfather, survived The Battle of the Blue Licks, near Lexington, Kentucky, on August 19, 1782, an Indian skirmish sometimes called "The last battle of the Revolution." "While crossing (the river) I heard a dreadful screaming and yelling, which proceeded from a number of Indians...tomahawking our men," he wrote. He ran, with an Indian in pursuit. "I found I must fight or die...I threw myself behind a log...This gave me a chance to take aim and fire. He (the Indian) staggered out of my sight and troubled me no more." Two days later he made it to the fort at Lexington, Kentucky. He owned five slaves.

MAJOR HERMAN BOWMAR SR., Moo's great-grandfather. From the *Frankfort Yeoman,* January, 1856: "In 1791 when Kentucky, impatient of the fierce and bloody incursions of the surrounding tribes of Indians, resolved by a united and vigorous blow to drive back the ruthless savages and establish the security of her homes and firesides, (Major Bowmar) was among the first to respond to the call...He was promoted to the office of Adjutant General and distinguished himself by his gallantry in the memorable and decisive battle fought against the Indians by the hardy riflemen under command of General Anthony Wayne, in August 1794, at Fallen Timbers near Toledo, Ohio." Major Bowmar, of Versailles, went on to serve three terms as sheriff of Woodford County, seven years as a judge and two terms in the Kentucky Senate. He ran for Congress as a Democrat to succeed the renowned Henry Clay, but was defeated by the Whig candidate. He was listed in the 1810 census as one of the largest slave-owners in Woodford County. Aitchee, Moo's older brother and the family scribe, assures us that Major Bowmar "was most kind to his slaves and watched over them with care."

His son, DR. JOSEPH HAMILTON DAVIESS BOWMAR, Moo's great-uncle, gave up the practice of medicine after marrying a Louisiana woman in 1838. He farmed his way into Louisiana antebellum plantation aristocracy. "We had 160 acres of land and ten or twelve slaves as a beginning," he wrote. "In 1861 when the war broke out we had 3,500 acres, worth an average of $50 per acre and about 100 slaves, with stock of mules and horses...At the beginning of the war we were rich.

At the end of the war we were poor indeed." After the Confederate defeat he moved to Vicksburg, Mississippi and went into the real estate business, riding his horse, Old Bloom, to work every day. He became a close friend and business associate of Jefferson Davis, the former president of the Confederacy. According to family journals, Bowmar represented Davis and his brother, Joseph E. Davis, in a successful bid to regain possession of their Mississippi plantation, which had been seized by Union forces.

ROBERT BOWMAR, one of Moo's many uncles, sneaked out of the house one night in July 1862, traveled from Versailles to Georgetown, Kentucky, and enlisted in the Confederate Army, under General John Hunt Morgan. Bowmar was thrust into combat immediately, acquitting himself bravely in three battles as Morgan's cavalry fought its way into Tennessee. But his captain discovered that he was only fifteen, two months short of the army's minimum age. He wired Robert's parents the welcome news that their son would be coming home. Robert's father waited up that night to welcome his son. At 4am a wagon clattered up, bearing a coffin. Just before leaving for home, young Robert Bowmar had been shot and killed when a comrade's gun accidentally fired.

CAPTAIN JOSEPH MARSHALL BOWMAR, Maw's father, was cited by the Confederate government for bravery after suffering severe wounds in the Battle of Green River Bridge, a Kentucky bloodbath won by Union forces on the symbolically significant date of July 4, 1863. Bowmar was imprisoned in Ohio with his commander, the same General Morgan. He was released two years later and served briefly as a bodyguard for President Jefferson Davis. Back in Versailles after the war, he worked as a banker and played the violin. He came down with tuberculosis and moved with his family to Texas, seeking dry air. But he died of TB in June 1889. Maw (Fanny Bowmar), one of four sisters, was nine years old, the same age Moo was when he lost his father..

On the moral front, HERMAN BOWMAR JR., Moo's grandfather, wrote a disturbing note to his son, Daniel Mayes Bowmar, on May 24, 1863, about a black acquaintance: "I regret extremely to inform you that your particular friend Arbuckle has made an abortive attempt to back slide…(He) had become fascinated with the charms of Amanda

Gatewood. He went over the way and told her my women were absent and I wished to see her. She came over and he met her in (sic) the porch and told her it was himself that desired to have a little private chat with her and invited her to his sleeping apartments…telling her that they could have a great satisfaction over thar (sic)…She fled…I let Arbuckle know that as soon as you returned I would have him tried before the African Church for entertaining such unholy desires."

In 1907 Moo, Maw and their daughter Charlotte, then two years old, left St. Paul and moved back to Versailles, reuniting with their large families and raising the town's population to about 2,340. Moo's older brothers, Aitchee and Dan, were there, running *The Woodford Sun*. Maw's sisters, Catherine and Elizabeth, spent their lives in Versailles, where Catherine, who never married, supervised an orphans' home and Elizabeth married George Fishback, a farmer just down McCracken Pike from a fine bourbon distillery, and raised two sons and a daughter. Alden and I called Catherine "Ta-a" and Elizabeth "Eiwees"—I don't know why. We would visit as little children, in the late 1930's and early '40's. I remember Eiwees beginning dinner preparations by grabbing a chicken from their flock, wringing its neck and cutting off its head. We helped churn milk to make butter.

Versailles was and is in the heart of the central Kentucky bluegrass, home to wealthy horse breeders and a hub for horse shows, foxhunts and other pastimes that carry forward traditions of the landed English gentry. Early Virginians eagerly embraced this model of rural gentility and passed it on to Kentucky, which was settled largely by Virginians seeking greener pastures to the west. Moo's ancestors moved to Kentucky from Pittsylvania County, Virginia (near Danville) in 1779, and settled in Woodford County ten years later.

The horse gentry formed the upper crust of Woodford County, and still does. England's Queen Elizabeth, a lifelong devotee of fine thoroughbreds, visited Woodford's finest horse-breeding establishments in May 1986, putting up at William Farish's premier Lane's End Farm.

Several expansive farms were complimented by graceful mansions in Versailles, the county seat and trading center. The Bowmars were not of this elevation, and neither, decidedly, were ordinary farmers, who sometimes were at odds with the fox hunters and their baying hounds. From *The Woodford Sun*, June 14, 1900:

"Squire J.C. Hays tells us that a red fox visited his poultry yard Saturday and carried off 32 out of 37 young turkeys. Sunday, while he was at church, Reynard returned for the remaining five and stood his ground until beaten with a club by the colored cook...Several other farmers report heavy losses by foxes...A movement looking to the extermination of Br'er Fox is seriously threatened and this, of course, is liable to bring on a war with the fox hunters."

In 1907, Moo took a job in the wholesale coal business, leaving railroad work behind. He and Maw obviously intended to stay in Versailles, building a house next door to Aitchee's and joining in the town's church-centered social life. From *The Woodford Sun*, February 18, 1908:

"Mrs. Herman Bowmar entertained the Children's Missionary Society of the Methodist church and a few of their friends at her home last Thursday afternoon. Each member of the society was privileged to bring a friend. A very pleasant afternoon was spent. Two prizes were awarded from those giving the greatest number of correct answers to Bible questions..."

But in 1912 they moved to St. Louis, where Moo became general secretary of the Missouri Sunday School Association. I'm not sure why. Had the coal business failed? Was this a religious leaning inherited from his father? At any rate, the new job enabled him to travel to Europe in 1913 as a delegate to a church convention in Zurich, which he parlayed into a fast-action European tour. Rising at 5:15 to lengthen the sight-seeing days, he toured Pisa, Rome, Florence, Heidelberg, Frankfort, Cologne, Amsterdam, Brussels, Paris, Versailles ("Moulin Rouge night"), Edinburgh, London and a half-dozen other British cities. He read the Bible and he read classics: "Read Acts. Read Thackeray," his terse diary noted.

The ship docked in Boston. Moo was a leader. "First person through customs," he wrote. After a cruise years later, Moo hustled to the baggage collection area at the pier, leaving wife and daughter behind. They couldn't find him and asked a baggage handler for help. "Lady," the man said in a tired voice, "he's out on the street directing traffic."

Back home in St. Louis, Moo's job required more travel, as he toured the state speaking to church and YMCA groups. "Spoke thirty-eight times," he noted in a diary, as he drove to the

Missouri cities and towns of St. Joseph, Kansas City, Elmwood, Jasper County, Dent County, Salem, New Haven, Gasconade County, Ripley County, Carthage, Joplin, Kirkwood and Clayton.

Moo and Maw at Lake Geneva, Wisconsin, where the Missouri Sunday School Association had a summer camp. About 1915.

Through the Sunday School Association, Moo became acquainted with William H. Danforth, an avid Christian, outdoorsman, and business visionary. Nowadays we connect the word "entrepreneur" with high-tech innovators like Steve Jobs and Bill Gates. But Danforth's vision was more down to earth, reflective of his times. In the late nineteenth and early twentieth centuries, more than half of Americans lived on farms or in very small towns (the percentage is now less than two percent). Most farms were of small acreage and were powered almost entirely by animals. Looking for a business that could thrive even in the nationwide depression of the 1890's, Danforth, reasoning that "animals must eat year-round," tapped into farmers' needs for inexpensive horse and mule feeds of good quality— mixtures of corn, oats and molasses, initially stirred with a shovel on a warehouse floor.

The market was vast. For example, in 1900 horses numbered more than 20 million on U.S. farms and another 3.5 million in U.S. cities, where horses, not cars, crowded the streets. From *The Woodford Sun,* November 1, 1900:

"The automobile made its first appearance in Versailles last Friday. It was a wagon advertising Dr. Pierce's patent medicines and was propelled by gasoline. It attracted much attention."

Danforth called his feeds Purina Chows, picking up on the military word for food. In search of a flamboyant trademark, he recalled a poor woman in his childhood hometown of Charleston, Missouri, who used red—and-white checkerboard cloth to make clothes for the whole family. Danforth packaged his Chows in red-and-white checkerboard bags. He initially sold them to farmers along the Mississippi River. The red and white checkered bags of Purina Chows soon were recognized throughout rural America.

    Danforth also introduced a whole wheat cereal, employing a new milling technique that prevented rancidity. According to a company history, he approached a Dr. Everett Ralston, described as an eminent national spokesman on health and nutrition, for an endorsement. OK, said Dr. Ralston, but only if you name the cereal after me. Ralston got his name not only on the cereal box—Ralston Wheat Cereal—but also on the company, which became Ralston Purina.

William B. Mead

The Fake Dr. Ralston

This appears to be a rare case in which Danforth may have been hoodwinked, because there was in fact, no "Dr. Ralston." It was one of at least two pen names used by Albert Webster Edgerly, a noted racist crackpot, for his book "Life Building," which recommended whole wheat cereal—right down Danforth's alley. The rest of Edgerly's work was not. He claimed 800,000 followers for his kooky brainchild "Ralstonism," which he immodestly described as "the grandest movement that man is capable of establishing." He wrote eighty-two books, most of them under the pen name Edmund Shaftesbury. His writings advocated castration at birth of all "non-racial" (non-Caucasian) males, and recommended that young men, before picking brides, should try a probationary marriage to a woman of grandmotherly age. He created a language called "Adam-Man-Tongue" with a thirty-three-letter alphabet. He laid down strict dietary rules—no watermelons for Caucasians—and peculiar exercises which, he said, would empower readers with a "personal magnetism" that would give them control over the thoughts of others (and help with sex, too.). He founded his version of a utopian community in New Jersey. It failed.

At Purina, Danforth often hired men he knew through religious and outdoor activities. In 1920 he offered Moo, then still with the Sunday School Association, a job as a sales manager. Moo considered a competing offer from a larger firm. He chose Danforth and Purina. For a physically active hardworking Christian non-smoking teetotaler, it was a perfect fit.

More than half of American adults smoked back then, but smoking was prohibited in the Ralston Purina office, where employees enjoyed exercise breaks, not coffee breaks. Twice a day, trainers (to use a modern term) threw the windows open to let in fresh air and led the troops—from Danforth to Moo to clerks and secretaries—in calisthenics. When men arrived for work they hung up their suit coats and donned lightweight checkerboard sport coats—Moo chose a conservative blue check. At company conventions, checkered clothing prevailed, and farm animals made robust from a Purina diet often shared the stage, even at convention hotels. Employees and their wives sang:

Fight fight fight for Old Purina!
There is a Chow for every need!
Never let the battle stop
Keep the Checkerboard on top
Fight to keep Purina in the lead!

However corny that appears today, Danforth's enthusiasm was infectious, and led to an esprit de corps that pushed Ralston Purina forward. Today most of us recognize Purina dog and cat chows, but the company used to make a smorgasbord of Chows, sold mostly to farmers, for poultry, rabbits, goats (three varieties), cattle, dairy cows, hogs, horses, sheep, lambs, wildlife, game birds, wild birds, exotic animals, various zoo animals--and dogs and cats.

As the company prospered, Danforth offered a dozen or so executives the opportunity to buy stock. Moo was one of them. Danforth somehow struck a deal with a local bank to lend his executives much more money than they could cover with collateral. This was about 1925, when an American business executive might make $3,000 a year--$37,000 in 2010 dollars. (Even allowing for inflation, business executives were paid much less back then than they are today.)

Moo borrowed $40,000, many times his salary, tying his future and that of his family to Ralston Purina. The company grew. Donald Danforth succeeded his father as CEO in 1932 and put Moo in charge of the cereal department, which brought in robust profits that compensated for Depression-era losses in Chow sales to farmers. By the time Alden and I went to college in the early 1950's, Ralston stock paid the way. It was listed on the New York Stock Exchange in 1962, fueling more growth and paying college tuition for our children and, to a large extent, their children. Moo's cogent investment had grown into millions. "I was lucky," he said. He was not a man to brag, and he rarely mentioned his childhood hardships. "Why did your father die so young, Moo?" "He fell off a train." Next topic.

In 1924 Danforth founded the nonprofit American Youth Foundation with two summer camps for children, both still flourishing—Camp Miniwanca at Shelby, Michigan, and Camp Merrowvista at Tuftonboro, New Hampshire. The AYF espoused an ethical life evenly balanced among mental, physical, social and religious thoughts and activities—"the foursquare life."

For Danforth, it was a lifelong mission. In 1938 he recruited Moo to serve on the board of directors and honored him with an Indian name—Mojag, meaning "never silent"—Moo must have been outspoken. Danforth was Minisino, which meant "Tried Warrior." He visited Miniwanca every summer and sent the campers home with checkerboard shirts. Alden and I wore them proudly.

In 1956, when he was seventy-five years old, Moo was named chairman of the Foundation's Finance Committee. He handled the Foundation's investments, and became known for his investing skills. Friends often came to him for advice. Many of them were widows whose husbands had handled the family finances, in keeping with the times. As he aged, I often saw Moo poring over small-type Standard & Poor's stock reports with a magnifying glass. He tended to recommend utilities, which back then could be counted on for steady, secure dividends, and St. Louis companies he knew through his downtown connections.

St. Louis was a growing, prosperous city when Moo and Maw arrived in 1912, ranking fourth among U.S. cities in population behind only New York, Chicago and Philadelphia.

"Meet Me in St. Louis"—The Greatest of All World's Fairs

The city was still basking in the glory of the 1904 World's Fair, which celebrated the hundredth anniversary of the Louisiana Purchase. Sixty-three nations and forty-three states built exhibit pavilions, and more than nineteen million people walked or rode the seventy-five miles of roads and walkways, visiting more than 1,500 buildings. From Lion of the Valley, St. Louis, Missouri, 1764-1980, *by historian James Neal Primm:*

"Even to the sophisticate, the sheer beauty of the Louisiana Purchase Exposition was overwhelming. Henry Adams, whose enthusiasm for the Middle West and for St. Louis in particular was quite limited, wrote in The Education of Henry Adams:

'The world had never witnessed so marvelous a phantasm; by night Arabia crimson sands had never returned a glow half so astonishing, as one wandered among long lines of white palaces, exquisitely lighted by thousands on thousands of electric candles, soft, rich, shadowy, palpable in their sensuous depths...One enjoyed it with iniquitous rapture...'"

Helen Keller gave a lecture. "The Louisiana Purchase Exposition is a great manifestation of all the forces of enlightenment and all of man's thousand torches burning together," she said.

Pennsylvania sent the Liberty Bell. India erected a reproduction of the Taj Mahal, and Virginia of Thomas Jefferson's Monticello. "Primitive peoples" were in vogue, so the Philippines set

Come Back Moo

up a village of Negritos—small, headhunting people. Visitors also gawked at Ota Benga, a Congolese pygmy; Geronimo, the Apache war chief; and Beautiful Jim Key, the educated horse, who could spell, do simple arithmetic, and, claimed his promoters, recognize any Bible passage that mentioned a horse. A British army unit staged the Second Boer War twice a day, each episode climaxing when the Boer General Christiaan de Wet escaped on horseback by leaping from a height of thirty-five feet into a pool of water (you could buy a bleacher seat for a quarter).

William B. Mead

Main thoroughfare at the 1904 World's Fair, St. Louis

John Philip Sousa was there with his marches and his band. Thomas Edison attended. J.T. Stinson, a distinguished fruit specialist, introduced the phrase "An apple a day keeps the doctor away." Dr. Pepper was introduced. So, according to various claims, were waffle-style ice cream cones, hamburgers, hot dogs, peanut butter, iced tea and cotton candy.

A popular song, "Meet Me in St. Louis," was published in 1904, just as the Fair opened. It contributed to the Fair's romantic appeal and was revived four decades later by the hit movie musical, "Meet Me in St. Louis"—or "St. Louie," as it was always sung-- starring Judy Garland. While burnishing the city's image, the song also gave Americans the mistaken idea that St. Louisans refer to their city as "St. Louie." We do not, and do not like to hear it suggested. In fact, the "Louie" in the song is a man, and the name was repeated to make a catchy rhyme. Here's the verse:

> *"When Louie came home to the flat.*
> *He hung up his coat and his hat.*
> *He looked all around but no wifey he found*
> *So he said 'Where can Flossie be at?'*
> *A note on the table he spied.*
> *He read it just once, then he cried.*
> *It said, 'Louie dear, it's too tame for me here*
> *So I think I will go for a ride…'*
> *Then the familiar chorus:*

"Meet me in St. Louie, Louie, meet me at the fair.
Don't tell me the lights are shining, anyplace but there.
We can dance the hootchie-coochie
I will be your tootsie-wootsy.
If you will meet me in St. Louie, Louie
Meet me at the fair!"

Prohibition Adventures

Prohibition didn't bother the teetotaling Bowmars, but it stripped St. Louis of a major industry—brewing—and enraged the city's many beer-drinking Germans and wine-drinking Italians, not to mention the entire tippling populace. Two St. Louis brewers committed suicide. On December 31 1922, three prohibition agents raided a high-society New Year's Eve party at the ritzy Chase Hotel, sparking a riot of protest. Putting aside their manners, the partygoers bombarded the agents with saltshakers, knives, forks, dishes and glasses. The agents fled for their lives but not before one fired a shot that ricocheted off the ballroom floor and wounded a man as he danced with his wife. (The wound was minor. No one was arrested.)

The dry life was hard on visiting Europeans. Sergei Rachmaninoff announced that he couldn't keep an engagement with the St. Louis Symphony Orchestra unless provided with "a dozen bottles of genuine beer to drink." August A. Busch invited the famed composer and pianist to his palatial country home and sent him back downtown with the necessary provisions.

William B. Mead

Sergei Rachmaninoff. The famed musician would not perform without a supply of beer.

Back in Versailles, Kentucky, Moo's older brother, Aitchee, shared Moo's abhorrence of booze. He, like Moo, may have been scarred by their father's alcoholism. Aitchee was a fervent supporter of Prohibition and used his columns in The Woodford Sun to preach the gospel of temperance—a hard sell in the heart of bourbon country. Here's Aitchee taking on Kentucky Governor Augustus Owsley Stanley, who had invoked Jesus Christ in a speech opposing Prohibition. From The Woodford Sun, March 22, 1917:

"The Governor would invoke the spirit of Jesus Christ to protect the barroom! To my mind this is nothing short of blasphemous! The barroom has made more widows than the most bloodthirsty tyrant who ever cursed the earth…The barroom has clouded and ruined the lives of more orphans than any agency on earth…"

World War II lifted the St. Louis economy, as war industries powered industrial growth. St. Louis population peaked at 880,000 in the early 1950's. St. Louis was second only to Detroit in automobile manufacturing. But decades before (in 1876), St. Louis had signed away its own future by separating itself from surrounding St. Louis County, home of suburbia and wellspring of future tax sources. Decaying downtown industry started the city's decline. In the 1960's, school integration prompted thirty-four percent of the city's white population to leave, most of them to relatively prosperous suburbs such as Maplewood, Kirkwood, Webster Groves, University City and Clayton, the seat of

St. Louis County. By 2010, the city that had proudly ranked fourth in population a century before now ranked fifty-eighth, with 319,294 residents. The St. Louis metro area, broadly defined, ranked eighteenth, with total population of 2,812,896.

Jim Crow

Moo and Maw, born so soon after the Civil War, lived through the entire era of Jim Crow. It is hard, now, to understand how deep and universal racial prejudice used to be in the United States. The conventional wisdom held blacks to be mentally inferior, fit for only menial work, shiftless, lazy, frequently objects of scorn and derision. Major companies, North and South, rarely considered blacks for white collar positions.

American newspapers, from *The New York Times* to the *Birmingham News*, largely ignored the black people in their cities, covering "Negro News" only in connection with heinous crimes and minstrel entertainment. White baseball fans today have read much more about Satchel Paige and Cool Papa Bell than did whites when these great stars were playing in the Negro leagues. They were absent from the sports pages of white newspapers, including the liberal *New York Times* and *St. Louis Post-Dispatch*, which filled their newsrooms with white editors and reporters.

Come Back Moo

Sportsman's Park, home of the Cardinals of the National League and St. Louis Browns of the American League, was one of only two segregated stadiums in major league baseball (The other was Griffith Stadium in Washington, D.C.). Blacks sat in the right field pavilion (so called) behind a screen. Injustice? As a child, I never gave it a thought. Like most people, I accepted the status quo.

So did most blacks. White parents had no qualms about letting their children, like Alden and me, ride streetcars into the largely black neighborhood where Sportsman's Park was located. The stadium was desegregated by the time Jackie Robinson joined the Brooklyn Dodgers in 1947 as the first black player in the major leagues, though many blacks continued to sit in the pavilion. I was surprised to hear St. Louis blacks cheering for the Dodgers. I was thirteen and utterly lacking in social awareness.

Neighborhoods and schools were segregated in our pristine suburb, Webster Groves. In much of Webster Groves, and in much of the country, discriminatory neighborhood covenants—laws written into real estate contracts, eventually outlawed—forbade selling a house to a black or a Jew. Douglas High School was all-black and was located in a residential area called North

William B. Mead

Webster, home of many blacks who worked for white residents and businesses.

In 1949, the city of Webster Groves opened a big, lovely municipal swimming pool. That July, three local blacks showed up for a swim. They were turned away, told the pool was for whites only. One of the blacks was Benny Gordon Jr., who had served in an all-black tank battalion in World War II, earning two bronze stars among other decorations. Gordon and other local blacks hired a lawyer and filed a lawsuit challenging the city's insistence on segregating the swimming pool.

This was five years before the Supreme Court ruling that outlawed public school segregation and more than a decade before Martin Luther King's March on Washington. The Webster Groves blacks were plowing new ground. They won; on December 18, 1950, a federal judge ruled that the city was violating the rights of the plaintiffs and "others of the Negro race" under the Fourteenth Amendment.

Rather than integrating the pool, the city closed it—a harbinger of "Massive Resistance" policies used by Southern states to avoid school integration almost a decade later. The City Council explained that "mixed swimming" would cause a drop in attendance, perhaps forcing the pool to lose money. Besides, said the Council, there were "parents' fears for the safety of their children."

The Council suggested opening the pool three days for whites to every one day for blacks. Instead, the pool remained closed. In 1953 voters elected a new mayor and a new city council. The pool opened that summer, for whites and blacks. There were no incidents, and in 1956, just a year after the Supreme Court's 1955 ruling, Webster Groves integrated its public schools.

Moo was the very epitome of human decency, yet through all this, I don't remember him criticizing any facet of the local racial divide. As a white man, of course, he benefitted. More important, I think, was that like most people, black and white, he accepted things as they were—the status quo. It was not until the civil rights marches and demonstrations of the 1960's that Americans fully realized the evils of Jim Crow.

A Deadly Race Riot

Things had been worse. In 1916, St. Louis voters overwhelmingly passed a law mandating racial segregation of housing, churches and dance halls. Courts threw it out, but a year later a murderous race riot broke out in East St. Louis, Illinois, just across the Mississippi River. Striking white workers at the Aluminum Ore Company were enraged when management brought

William B. Mead

in black laborers from the South—strikebreakers, or in union parlance, "scabs."

I found the newspaper accounts that follow in *Lion of the Valley: St. Louis, Missouri, 1764-1980*, by the late James Neal Primm, a distinguished history professor at the University of Missouri-St. Louis.

From *The St. Louis Republic*, July 3, 1917, page 1:

"100 SLAIN, 500 HURT IN RACE RIOT
6 E. ST. LOUIS BLOCKS BURNED
BY MOB TO WIPE OUT BLACKS
Negroes Are Beaten, Burned, Shot and Drowned
by Men, Women, Girls and Boys..."

Policemen stood by, or even joined in the carnage. From *The St. Louis Post-Dispatch*, July 3, 1917, by reporter Carlos Hurd:

"For an hour and a half last evening I saw the massacre of helpless Negroes at Broadway and Fourth Streets in downtown East St. Louis where a black skin was a death warrant...

"I saw man after man, with his hands raised pleading for his life, surrounded by groups of men...who knew nothing about him except that he was black—and saw them administer the historic sentence of intolerance, death by stoning...

"'Get a nigger!' was the slogan, and it was varied by the recurrent cry, 'Get another!'"

Come Back Moo

Hundreds of blacks fled across the Eads Bridge to St. Louis, where police protected them; St. Louis did itself proud. Most of the refugees never returned to East St. Louis.

From *Champion: Joe Louis, Black Hero in White America*, an acclaimed biography of the great boxer written by our son, Chris Mead, in 1985:

"Historians recognize W.E.B DuBois and A. Philip Randolph as the most important black leaders of the 1930s; white Americans of that era would have been hard pressed to recognize their names…DuBois and Randolph simply did not appear in white newspapers."

All this was true when I was growing up, in the American Midwest of the 1940's and '50's. Imagine how hard racial attitudes and stereotypes were in small-town Kentucky when Moo and Maw were growing up, in the late nineteenth and early twentieth centuries. Slavery was within the memory of older residents, and slavery had flourished in Woodford County because two of the region's principal crops, burley tobacco and hemp, required lots of hard, hand labor. Slaves, of course, labored for free.

Crime was rarely heinous in Woodford County, but Negro perpetrators were always identified, sometimes in highly critical terms. From *The Woodford Sun*, April 13, 1889:

William B. Mead

"KILLED A HORSE"

On Wednesday night of last week two negroes went to the place of Mr. David Holden, on the Crawfish turnpike, and cut the throat of an old gray buggy mare belonging to Mrs. Holden, which they then skinned…The hide was sold by the fiends to a colored dealer in Versailles." (The "fiends" were arrested, and confessed.)

The same newspaper page featured an "In and About Versailles" column listing marriages, births and entertainment items such as these:

"Latest 'coon songs' and local jokes at Society Minstrels Friday night…The Society Minstrels will be the greatest amusement event that Versailles has had in many years—65 Versailles people in grand blackface overture. A big cake walk, pickaninny dance and chorus…" ("Coon" was a derogatory term for a black. A "cake walk" was a dance, originally performed by black slaves on plantations. "Pickaninny" was a condescending term for a black child. The main purpose of blackface minstrel shows was to poke fun at blacks.)

My grandparents had to climb their way out of these Jim Crow assumptions and traditions. They did, ahead of their times, but they started from the bottom. Moo used to tell "Negro jokes" on the very informal guest talent shows at Fair Hills Resort in Minnesota, where our family spent many wonderful vacations. Examples:

"Is you comin' to prayer meetin' tonight, Brudder Heidt?"

"Well, Preacher, I dunno. To tell you do troof, I is got a complimentary ticket to de Darktown Minstrels. Religion is aw right, Preacher; but a good minstrel show—"

The parson looked stern. "Brudder Heidt, dere won't be no minstrel shows in Heaven!"

"Oh! Den in dat case, I'll just go to de show tonight, while my ticket's good."

One more:

"Say, nigger," his wife regarded him angrily, "ebber since I married you, all you does is sit aroun' dis house, an' exercisin' yo feet by puttin' one dem on top of de udder on my mahogany table. Don't you ebber feel any ambition?"

"Lawd, baby, I feels ambition when I's sittin' around, honey; dat's why I sits aroun'. But jes' as soon as I starts to go to work, I gits plumb discouraged."

Fair Hills guests, all white, all decent people, mostly from the Twin Cities of Minneapolis and St. Paul, looked forward to Moo's jokes. There were no gasps of disapproval until Moo caught himself. He abruptly stopped telling racial jokes, on the resort stage and elsewhere, and he expressed regret at ever telling them. As a young man, he told us, he once refused to shake the hand of a black man to whom he was introduced. It haunted him; years later he looked up the black man and apologized.

Moo's oldest brother, Aitchee, the country editor, was an inspiration. Think of the editor of a small-town Southern newspaper writing this editorial in 1939, when anti-Semitism was widespread. Many companies wouldn't hire Jews, many hotels wouldn't admit them, and prominent leaders like Henry Ford openly blamed Jews for the ills of the world.

Quoting a letter published in *The Louisville Times*: "The Jewish race perhaps unconsciously leave the impression that they think theirs is a superior race of people. There is no place in past or present history to confirm this theory."

Aitchee's response, in *The Woodford Sun*, July 20, 1939:

"This is a most astonishing statement. There is everything in history to confirm the idea that the Jews are a superior race...Haunted, hounded, robbed, murdered, through all the years, did the Jews lose their strong personality, their high intelligence, their unusual character, the will to survive? They did not...Vocations which make for human welfare and alleviate human misery have always attracted the Jew…Who is the most brilliant scientist in the world? Einstein, a Jew…Is there any other race which has preserved its mental, moral and physical stamina—in the highest degree—under nearly eighteen hundred years of steady mistreatment, continuous attack, persecution and accumulated horrors? If the Jews have not proven themselves to be one of the world's superior races, I can't imagine what test you would apply to ascertain superiority."

Moo's Vacations

Back to Moo and Ralston Purina, here's another creed that Moo certainly lived by and may have composed. I found it in his diaries:

"An executive who is always busy is usually doing a lot of stuff that a youthful assistant could do just as well in half the time."

Moo took vacations of astounding length, beyond the dreams of today's executives, much less those working in the straightened circumstances of the 1930's and 1940's. He kept minute track of vacation travel expenses and jotted it all down in his diaries. (Numbers in parentheses are translations into 2013 dollars.)

"England, 1936, 6/30 to 8/9--$1,782 ($29,811). Great Britain 1938, 7 weeks 4 ½ days, $2,186 ($36,051).

South America 1940, 7 weeks, $3,005 (49,911). West (U.S) 1941, 6 weeks, 5 people, $2,706 ($42,805)."

At age seven, I was one of the five people on the Western trip, along with Moo and Maw, Mother and Alden. Traveling by train, the norm back then, we visited Yellowstone, Bryce Canyon, Zion, the Grand Canyon, Yosemite, Lake Louise and other famous sites, as well as a few cities—Seattle, San Francisco and Los Angeles, where we visited an alligator and ostrich farm. We traveled first class—Pullmans—and stayed in the famous park lodges. Not a bad summer vacation for a rising third-grader.

Moo loved to recall how he managed to take so much time off from work. The Danforths were enthusiastic travelers, so Moo saw an opening. During an annual salary review, Moo, reporting excellent profits from the cereal business year after year, told Danforth: "Frances and I want to do some traveling. You don't care how much vacation I take, do you, as long as I keep the numbers up?" OK, said Mr. Danforth, and Moo cogently asked him to dictate a note to that effect so Moo could show it to the startled treasurer and personnel manager. Then he started taking these long trips, to the envious amazement of his colleagues.

While traveling, for business or pleasure, Moo read extensively and kept up a voluminous correspondence, mostly by postcards. Diary notations of a 1940 trip list thirty-eight postcard recipients from Donald Danforth to me (I was six). After retiring from Purina in 1945, Moo started buying the family groceries. He introduced himself to the staff at the neighborhood Kroger supermarket and, when out of town, struck up a correspondence with the butchers, who had learned exactly how to cut steaks and roasts for Mr. Bowmar. They taped his postcards to the butcher counter.

Maw, Moo, Mother and companions in Egypt, 1952

When they weren't traveling overseas, Moo and Maw would travel to Florida for two weeks in the winter and

William B. Mead

to Fair Hills Resort, outside Detroit Lakes, Minnesota, for eight weeks in the summer.

Fair Hills

Most resorts emphasize luxury. Fair Hills emphasizes fun. It's been doing that for almost a century, all under the Kaldahl family. Oh, it's plenty comfortable. Your cabin is made up every day, you're well fed breakfast, lunch and dinner, and if you have a complaint a Kaldahl will quickly appear to set things right.

But you won't. You and your kids will be too busy enjoying lovely Pelican Lake, playing golf or tennis, entering tournaments, preparing a goofy act for the Tuesday night Hootenanny or the Thursday night talent show. (Disclaimer: I own no stock in Fair Hills. But Dave Kaldahl has been one of my best friends since 1938, when Mother, Alden and I first traveled to Fair Hills. I was four. Alden and Dave were five.)

You think I might be off my rocker about this place because we've been there, with four generations, for thirty-some summers? Well, we have company. Mary Linnerooth Peterson first came with her parents in 1945 and later worked as a Fair Hills waitress. She still comes, with her children and their families. Bruce Meyer first showed up sixty-two years ago, and still comes with children and grandchildren.

Come Back Moo

The Schupps of Des Moines first vacationed at Fair Hills in 1966. Their son Dan married the boss, or at least the boss-to-be, Beth Kaldahl. She's now the general manager. She also sings with her Dad, Dave, and two other men in the barbershop quartet. Her brother, Steve, handles maintenance, and sister Lisa supervises landscaping. Their Mom, Barb, Dave's wife of fifty-nine years, leads energetic early risers on a brisk two-mile morning walk. Barb then jumps in the pool and leads guests in water aerobics. Barb is eighty-one (as of 2013). So is Dave, who opens the office-store at 6am and starts the coffee pot. The dining room opens for breakfast at 8am. Dave cooks the eggs or French toast, for 250 resort guests. He used to build cabins in the off-season. He sings and plays the saxophone.

I could go on, because dozens of families, literally, have vacationed at Fair Hills for generations, worked at Fair Hills as they grew up—my brother, Alden, was a lawn boy—and married Fair Hills sweethearts. We now live in Maryland, outside Washington, D.C., where most people head for the ocean. I view Fair Hills as a precious Midwestern secret. (A week at Fair Hills costs about $1,100 for an adult, $600 for a child. That's American plan and includes lodging, meals, golf, boats and all activities.)

William B. Mead

Fair Hills News   MARCH, 1967

Our HONORED GUESTS for '67

The Burkitts, The Bowmars And The Meads

Each year we honor some of our guests that have vacationed with us the longest, and this year it is a family. The Bowmars have been with us all summer for 22 years. Their daughter, Mrs. Charlotte Burkitt has vacationed at Fair Hills for 26 years . . . usually for at least a month . . . while her husband Bob has been a regular guest since their marriage about 10 years ago. Bill Mead, the Bowmar's grandson and Mrs. Burkitt's son, vacationed here as a child and now brings his wife Jennifer and their three children, Christopher, Andrew and Megan. Not pictured is Bill's brother Alden who also comes up every year. Alden and Bill along with myself formed the "Terrible Trio" here at Fair Hills. They spent all summer here many moons ago when we were growing up together.

Bill is with UPI in Detroit Michigan, Alden is a professor at the University of Minnesota, and the Burkitts and Bowmars live in Glendale, Missouri.

After so many years of friendship, it is always a real pleasure for me to see them all again each year . . . Bill and Alden . . . two boyhood chums . . . Mrs. Burkitt, who let us play countless games of "Zoom" in our wet bathing suits in her cabin . . . Mr. Bowmar, who is our official weatherman, clock setter, and most important, our official greeter of new guests and old. Bob the inventor and suggestor of many good ideas for safety and convenience here at Fair Hills. Jennifer, with her Virginia drawl, trying to keep Chris, Andy and Megan in line . . . and last, but not least, Mrs. Bowmar, whom we all love for her sweet and gentle nature.

Come Back Moo

Moo and Maw spent their summer vacations on Georgian Bay in Canada until World War II made travel difficult. They then started joining us at Fair Hills. Here's the Fair Hills family roster, all on hand for multiple decades: Moo and Maw; Mother and Dad (our stepfather, Bob Burkitt, who courted Mother on a creaky porch swing in 1943 while Alden and I, supposedly asleep, listened inside); Alden, his wife Karin, and occasionally one or two of their three children; me, my wife Jenny, and our three kids, Chris, Andy and Meagan.

Through the 1940's and '50's, Fair Hills had just one telephone. Moo didn't use it. Having delegated authority to his assistant, Moo saw no reason to check in with the Ralston Purina office. He was on *vacation*. Before breakfast, Moo would swim way out on Pelican Lake, float on his back for ten minutes, then swim in for a cold shower. He and Maw canoed across the lake after breakfast, and he'd take a dip before lunch and again before dinner. When a mild heart attack prompted Moo's doctor to caution him against such long and vigorous swims, Moo switched to golf. He and Maw walked nine holes after breakfast and again after lunch.

Moo and Maw at Fair Hills Resort, about 1965

For all his vigorous outdoor life, Moo's favorite recreation was reading. Moo picked up a book anytime he had an hour to himself, and he made sure he had many such hours. My most vivid picture of Moo recalls him sitting in his rocking chair, positioned to benefit from sunshine, with a book in his hands, while Maw read or played solitaire nearby.

Come Back Moo

Moo's reading interests were broad. A 1940 diary entry includes books by Stewart Edward White, a popular and prolific writer of the outdoors, particularly the American West; Samuel Pittingill, a former congressman from Indiana and a leading critic of President Franklin Roosevelt's New Deal; Louis Bromfield, agrarian reformer, author of thirty best-sellers and winner of the Pulitzer Prize; and Evelyn Eaton, a prominent Canadian writer.

He devoured the classics. An inventory of books he owned at his death, in 1973, includes the works of Charles Dickens (seventeen volumes), George Eliot (eight), Rudyard Kipling (ten), O. Henry (thirteen), William Shakespeare (twenty), William Makepeace Thackeray (thirty-two) and dozens of other works, on religion, history, biography, travel, nature, and fiction. Moo disliked debt, but as a young man he was so anxious to acquire a complete set of Thackeray's work that he bought it on time, startling his young wife. In choosing books to read to Alden and me, Moo's bookshelf, and knowledge, always yielded a variety of wonderful choices. On our own, we read Batman and Superman comic books, graduating to boys' adventure books—*The Hardy Boys*—and to the boys' baseball books of John R. Tunis—*The Kid from Tomkinsville*.

William B. Mead

Maw finished high school but Moo had to quit school after eighth grade, so he set out to educate himself, traveling, reading voluminously and avoiding entertainments that they didn't consider uplifting. Moo and Maw went to plays, never movies. Nowadays film is respected as an art form, but back then it was not. Moo took Maw with him to business conventions in New York so they could attend hit plays every evening. They would come home raving about Alfred Lunt and Lynn Fontanne, an illustrious husband-and-wife acting team, and other outstanding performers.

After retiring from Ralston Purina in 1945, Moo imposed seasonal schedules on his reading—serious works most of the year, detective novels in the summer. Moo loved order. He and Maw got up, ate meals, and went to bed at the same time every day, with a bedtime snack of two Ritz crackers, washed down with Metamucil. Monday's dinner entrée was the same as last Monday's, and if we ate ham last Tuesday you could count on a ham dinner this Tuesday, too. After he retired in 1945, they also napped on schedule.

At age forty Mother remarried, to a man ten years her senior. Bob Burkitt courted Mother slowly. Noone said so, but he was a short step beneath her socially and a big step beneath Moo as a breadwinner. When Bob proposed, Mother asked Moo's advice, and got a strong endorsement. "He may never make a lot of money," Moo told her, "but he's a fine man." Indeed he was. They enjoyed more than thirty years together. Alden and I started calling him "Dad" after only a month or two, and for decades we enjoyed him as stepfather and golfing partner.

Bob Burkitt Invents a Better Mousetrap

"If a man can write a better book, preach a better sermon, or make a better mousetrap than his neighbor, though he builds his house in the woods the world will make a beaten path to his door."—Ralph Waldo Emerson.

Dad—Bob Burkitt—was a tinkerer and entrepreneur. His company—named "Piper" after the fictional Pied Piper, who entranced rats and mice with his piped music and led them away—made poisons for rats, mice, gophers, moles, ants and roaches. For a while our basement housed caged rats on which Dad would try his latest mixture. One day he roasted a new batch in the kitchen oven, used by Mother to roast chickens and bake cookies. It stank and pushed Mother over the edge. The rats and their poisons were forever banished. Alden and I kept the pet mice Dad had given to us but we were negligent in feeding them, and eventually one mouse ate the other and escaped.

The Piper company was small, selling to grocery and hardware stores only in Missouri and surrounding states, and Dad, on a shoestring, did some of the selling himself. Much of his territory was rural, and farmers told him that his baits, as he called them, would not tempt rural rats because they feasted on farm grains. What rats were looking for, one told Dad, was water.

The light dawned. Dad invented the better mousetrap, and rattrap. It was made of aluminum, with a depression into which you poured water. The trigger was a flat piece of aluminum over the water, with holes into which the rodent would poke his nose. WHAM! Down came the spring-loaded steel clamp, just as in a regular trap. Dead rodent.

Dad lacked money for advertising, so he cleverly hired a young public relations man, who touted Dad as the man who built a better mousetrap. The PR agent got Dad booked on a couple of network television shows, where he demonstrated his invention. This was about 1948. We didn't have a television set—lots of families didn't back then-- so we proudly watched Dad at a neighbor's house.

Just as Emerson predicted, the world beat a path to Dad's door. Orders rolled in and aluminum traps rolled out. But then, disturbingly, many rolled back. Dad had hired a local minnow-bucket manufacturer to make the traps, and he used a weak aluminum alloy. When the spring-loaded steel trigger came down—hard—the soft aluminum trap tended to fold up, into a V. Dad and the minnow-bucket man geared up to fix the problem with a stronger alloy. But then the Korean War broke out, in 1950. To make warplanes, the U.S. government needed all the aluminum American companies could produce. There was nothing left over for rodent traps.

Dad got the word at work one day. He had borrowed all the money he could to get his project off the ground and moving. He had no way to repay the loans. Mom and Dad were not rich—just to help make ends meet, the spare bedroom upstairs was rented out to a school teacher, who had to share a bathroom with Alden and me.

As Mother later told us, Dad came home so distraught she feared for him. The family faced financial ruin. She called Moo. Dad had never asked him for a penny and didn't want to now. Moo came over, got the story out of Dad, wiped out the loan in one swipe, and never mentioned it again, not wanting Dad to feel humbled. Years before Moo had rescued Mother, Alden and me from the prospect of a bleak life, and now he had done the same for Dad—by extension, for all of us.

The rattrap fiasco wasn't Dad's first brush with bad luck. In the late 1920's, well before Mother knew him, he operated a music school in St. Louis. His students included Helen Traubel, later a star with the Metropolitan Opera in New York. But the Depression was not kind to businesses like music schools, and Dad's enterprise folded.

Come Back Moo

When Mother married Bob in 1944, I was ten years old and Alden was twelve. We moved with them to their house, two blocks from the Bowmar home. But Moo and Maw implored us to spend our weekends with them. We did so, very happily, all through our high school and college years. At a stage in life when many couples are glad to enjoy privacy as empty-nesters, Moo and Maw still wanted their grandsons with them. When Alden and I got our driver's licenses at sixteen, Moo let us borrow the older of his two Oldsmobiles one evening a week and one afternoon. We cut their grass and raked their leaves—a positive trade from our standpoint.

Dad died in 1985 at age eighty-eight after ten years of advanced senility—alzheimer's in modern terminology. Gradually, Mother mourned him less and mourned openly for her first husband—Chet, father of Alden and me. She had been a young woman deeply in love and her happiness was jerked out from under her.

Brains for Breakfast

From our childhood, Sunday breakfast was the best meal of the week, and preparations began the evening before, when Moo and Maw made maple syrup from the Canadian maple sugar they ordered by mail. The menu, a combination of Kentucky and St. Louis German traditions, featured Maw's corn meal battercakes—tiny thin pancakes far superior to anything Aunt Jemima or a pancake house could provide—and eggs scrambled with calves' brains. People nowadays blanch at the thought of eating brains, but calves brains are considered a delicacy in some German, Austrian, Turkish and Moroccan restaurants. In St. Louis, a beer and a fried brain sandwich used to be a favorite workingman's lunch at a few old-country bars.

Bowmar home cuisine was standard American excellent, with Southern leanings but no trace of gourmet striving. But when traveling abroad Moo and Maw enthusiastically enjoyed foreign specialties unknown to most Americans. In 1952 they took Alden and me on a grand summer-long tour of Europe, first class all the way. We were amazed at their dining choices. Escargot? *Alden! Moo and Maw are eating snails!* Putting up in Paris at the Plana Athenee, one of the world's great hotels with cuisine to match, Alden and I ate steak and French fries every night.

That trip cost $11,246, according to Moo's meticulous calculations--$98,681 in 2013 dollars!

Moo was a big benefactor of the First Congregational Church of Webster Groves. He and Maw attended services every Sunday though he gradually became skeptical of Christian beliefs. "The Church does good work in the community," he said, explaining his continued support.

When not traveling overseas, Moo and Maw drove to Fair Hills every summer, leaving home in mid-June and staying until just short of Labor Day. As children, Alden and I drove with them. The trip was 812 miles, and took us through numerous cities and towns—the Interstate Highway System was yet to be built—as well as hundreds of miles of gently rolling farmland, most of it planted in corn. Moo and Maw believed in eating meals and staying nights at the best hotels. Moo took a shine to a waitress at Hotel Iowa in Keokuk and made it a point to stay there and ask for her at dinner, year after year. In Minneapolis, The Curtis Hotel was, in Bowmar estimation, the Waldorf-Astoria. The third day's drive took us through rural Minnesota—Lake Wobegon country-- to Fair Hills. Along the way, Alden and I read comic books in the back seat and kept an eye out for the entertaining jingles advertising Burma-Shave.

William B. Mead

Burma-Shave

Burma-Shave introduced its billboard advertising campaign in 1925. The signs were in series of six, red and white, far enough apart so a driver had time to digest each one. Examples:

A peach
Looks good
With lots of fuzz
But man's no peach
And never wuz
Burma-Shave

Highway safety messages were often featured:
Hardly a driver
Is now alive
Who passed
On hills
At 75
Burma-Shave

Burma-Shave sales soared, and the brand soon ranked second among brushless shaving creams, which back then came in tubes, not aerosols. But just as older highways had enabled the brand to prosper, newer highways killed it. On interstate highways, drivers drove too fast to digest a series of six signs. By 1963 the signs were gone, and soon Burma-Shave was gone with them.

Henry Wallace

Less spectacular were signs identifying fields of corn as Pioneer Hi-Bred. You still see them today. The first version of this high-yielding hybrid corn was developed in 1926 by Henry A. Wallace, a pioneering Iowa agronomist and farm-journal editor. For seed corn, farmers used to use kernels from cobs that looked the best, figuring that the prettier the seed corn the better the quality and yield.

But Wallace observed that this theory didn't work. Besides, he said, most field corn is fed to hogs, which didn't care what their feed looked like. So he crossed strains in various combinations until he came up with a seed corn that produced great big yields. He named it Pioneer Hi-Bred and it soon swept the market.

Henry Wallace, secretary of agriculture and future vice president, testifying before a Congressional committee.

William B. Mead

Wallace was a Republican, but President Franklin D. Roosevelt appointed him U.S. Secretary of Agriculture in 1933 and Wallace became an enthusiastic booster of New Deal programs. In 1940 Roosevelt chose Wallace as his vice-presidential running mate. They were elected but Wallace's liberalism soon ran him afoul of more traditional Democrats. When Roosevelt ran for a fourth term in 1944 he dumped Wallace from the ticket in favor of another Midwesterner with a farm background — Senator Harry S Truman of Missouri. Roosevelt and Truman won, but 83 days later Roosevelt died, and Truman became president. Had Roosevelt not switched running mates, Henry A. Wallace would have become president.

Instead, Wallace slid to the left margin politically, praising the Soviet governments of Joseph Stalin and Vyacheslav Molotov and advocating racial integration in the U.S. He ran for president as a Progressive in 1948 but got only 2.4 percent of the popular vote. He returned to his agricultural experiments, developing a breed of chicken that laid so many good eggs it became the standard worldwide. A superior honeydew he developed for the Chinese is still known there as the "Wallace melon."

In 1950 Wallace acknowledged that he had been dead wrong in supporting the Soviet Union. He endorsed U.S. participation in the Korean War, and supported the reelection of President Dwight Eisenhower, a Republican, in 1956. In 1965 he died of Lou Gehrig's disease (amyotrophic lateral sclerosis).

Moo disapproved of smoking and gambling as well as drinking. He offered Alden and me a hundred dollars if we would refrain from smoking until we were twenty-one. Alden earned it. I failed, but neither Moo nor Maw called me to task. They just didn't give me the hundred dollars.

The Fair Hills store and office boasted two or three slot machines, as well as a soda fountain and plentiful supplies of candy bars, fish hooks, golf balls, Indian jewelry and such. Alden and I were forbidden to play the slots, most of which took nickels or dimes; a quarter machine was for high rollers.

I couldn't resist, and one fine day I hit three bells on a nickel machine that paid double. Three bells, doubled! Thirty-six nickels poured out. I itched to tell Moo and Maw, and figured his aversion to gambling would be overwhelmed by this great wealth—*one* nickel would buy a candy bar, a Coke or a single-scoop ice cream cone.

I was wrong. Sternly, Moo ordered me to invest every penny in War Stamps. This was during World War II, when everyone was encouraged to buy War Bonds, and children were given stamp books. A stamp cost a quarter, and once you filled your book with seventy-five stamps you got a War Bond worth $18.75, maturing ten years later at $25. No child, to my knowledge, ever stuck with this noble savings plan long enough to get a bond.

William B. Mead

A Fond History of Slot Machines

Slot machines were illegal in Minnesota, but lake resorts like Fair Hills badly needed the additional revenue during World War II, when gasoline rationing made it difficult for families to drive up north for vacations. So the state government let the reels spin until Governor Luther W. Youngdahl took office in 1947, vowing to rid Minnesota of slots. Opponents ridiculed Youngdahl as the "Sunday School governor," but he prevailed, and slot machines disappeared from Fair Hills. I was disappointed. Moo was glad.

Modern slot machines are electronic, providing various formats and lots of sound effects and visual glitz. Early slots, like those at Fair Hills, were mechanical. You didn't even plug them in, and the sound effect that made players happy was the roar and clink of coins shooting down the chute and dropping into the payoff tray. A typical machine returned about 75 cents for every dollar gambled. Today's electronic slot machines return 90 to 95 cents to the dollar; casino operators have learned that the higher payout ratio keeps gamblers playing, yielding more profit.

Charles Fey of San Francisco invented the mechanical three-reel slot machine in 1897 and slots quickly appeared by the thousands in saloons, pool halls, cafes, bowling alleys and other businesses. To get around anti-gambling laws, some slots paid off only in trade—i.e. three oranges earned you cigars or chewing gum instead of the traditional ten nickels or dimes. The Mills Novelty Company of Chicago, a leading slot manufacturer, offered a model so small and light—it weighed thirty-six pounds—that a bartender or deli clerk could quickly hide it under the counter if a cop showed up. It was called the "QT", as in doing something quietly, "on the QT." (You can buy one, nicely restored, on Rebslots.com or EBay for about $2,500.)

Bugsy Siegel, a notorious gangster, introduced slot machines to Las Vegas casinos in the late 1940s. He thought they would pass the time for women while their high-roller husbands shot craps. Instead, slots became every casino's most popular game, by far.

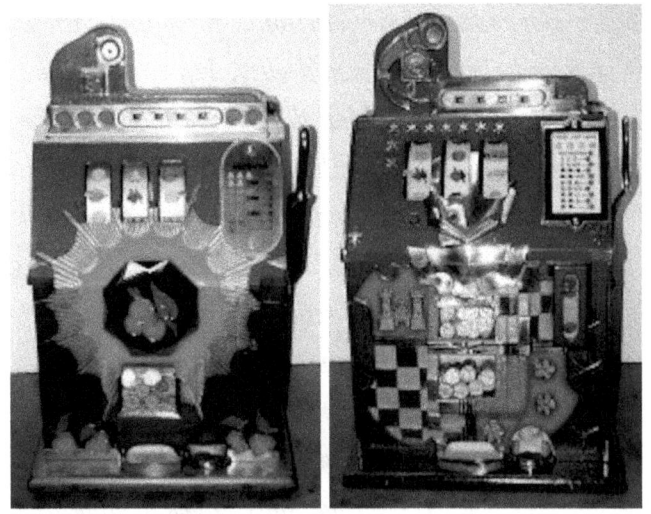

Mechanical slot machines. Fancy Designs like these were popular in the 1930's, 40's, and '50's.

Moo and Maw were the first ones in the Fair Hills dining room every day for every meal. As soon as they arrived for their first meal of the season Moo marched into the kitchen and greeted the cooks, many of whom worked at Fair Hills summer after summer and knew him well. (Cheryl Hoban , the present head chef, doesn't go back that far. She's cooked at Fair Hills for only thirty-seven years.)

Moo put salt on his grapefruit and pepper on his cantaloupe. He liked a slice of sharp cheddar on his apple pie. He and Maw insisted on bacon so crisp that "Bowmar bacon" was part of the waitress-and-cook vocabulary at Fair Hills, and remained so for years after Moo's death.

He and Maw took care to get acquainted with the waitresses—young women working their way through college, most of them from the farms and small towns of Minnesota and North Dakota. In his diaries Moo listed their names, which reflected the Scandinavian heritage of that region—Judy Kaldahl, Karen Eckholm, Joyce Helgeson, Shirley Gilbertson, JoAnn Doran, Mary Smedstad, Ruth Anderson, Carol Madison.

The nearest town, Detroit Lakes, was twelve miles from the resort and employees didn't have cars, the times and family traditions being much tighter than they are today. Two afternoons a week, on schedule, Moo, and usually Maw, drove into town for haircuts and shopping. They offered space in their Oldsmobile for four waitresses, and gradually learned which young women seemed to be particularly promising and came from the poorest families. Late every summer two or three Fair Hills waitresses would find checks in their mailboxes covering the next year's tuition. Moo was carrying forward the tradition that began with the benefactor of his own father—"Take it, and as you prosper, help every young man in his need, especially if you think as well of him as I do of you." (Moo preferred young women to young men.)

In 1953 Moo met a Fair Hills waitress who was to lead him to the second love of his life. Helju Aulik was poor, barely sustained by a scholarship at the University of Kansas. A college friend told her about Fair Hills, and she landed a waitress job—coveted summertime work in that era. At Fair Hills they called her "Esti," because she was a wartime refugee from Estonia, the tiny Baltic country ravaged in turn by the Germans and Soviets during and after World War II.

Paula Aulik, Moo's Second Love

The Auliks' experiences are best told in plain journalistic prose. The hardships and dangers they surmounted, and the courage they demonstrated, exceed any use of superlatives.

Helju, born in 1934, was the oldest of five Aulik children. Their father, Voldemar, was a police officer. Stalin's Soviet Russia invaded Estonia in June of 1940, quickly absorbing the tiny

William B. Mead

country. At least 100,000 Estonians were killed, mobilized into the Soviet army, or deported, probably to Siberia. Just a year later, Hitler's German army swept through the country, ousting the Soviets. The Estonian people were caught in a violent vise between two of history's cruelest regimes.

Helju, then seven, and her brother Arvo, two years younger, watched German soldiers trample the grain growing on their grandparents' farm. The family hid in a fruit cellar as the Germans set up a machine gun near their barn and another at a nearby vodka distillery. With automatic gunfire, the Germans raked the fields where Soviet soldiers were hiding. The next day the Aulik children's' father and grandfather, who had hidden in the woods during the massacre, hitched a horse to a sled and drove through their fields, loading dead Soviet solders and hauling them to a common grave dug by neighboring farmers. The sleds crushed the grain and the bodies dripped blood, ruining the crop.

German soldiers came to their farmhouse, demanding food. The Auliks set up a kettle, boiled eggs for the soldiers and gave them bacon. Miraculously, the family was not harmed, even though their pet German Shepherd, Tika, trained as a watchdog, slipped his leash one evening and killed a straggling Soviet soldier. Arvo, five years old, held a lantern while his father and grandfather buried the soldier and successfully disguised his grave.

On September sixth 1941 Helju's father, Voldemar, was sent with a special police unit to apprehend a band of Soviet terrorists, or guerillas, who were raiding Estonian farms, stealing food and *valuables, raping women and killing civilians. The Estonian policemen lacked camouflage uniforms. A sniper saw the gold braid on Aulik's hat and shot him through the head, killing him instantly. His wife, Paula, twenty-seven, found his body, scooped his brains back into his skull, cut off his bloodstained uniform and dressed him in a clean one for burial, and bicycled to a church where his body was taken. She assured the relative safety of her young family, and went to work.*

Voldemar Aulik, Paula's assassinated husband, lies on his bier surrounded by family, friends and Estonian police colleagues. A cloth covers the fatal head wound. Looking down at their father are Helju, 7; Inga, 6; and Arvo, 5. Paula, their mother, stands behind them holding Jaak, 13 months old.

William B. Mead

Paula got a job at a government office. Her younger sister, Vaike, helped care for the children. Cruel as the Germans were, they were better than the Soviets—who recaptured Estonia in 1944. Paula learned that the Auliks were on a Soviet wanted list. She took her children and moved into the woods, hiding within trellis teepees that were set up for climbing vines of peas and beans. The children sneaked out to pick mushrooms, strawberries and other edibles. Grandparents, aunts and uncles brought food.

Paula finagled a permit granting the Auliks space on a decrepit fishing boat, converted to accommodate people, that was to leave Tallinn, Estonia, for Poland, which was in German hands. Paula, her children and her younger sister, Vaika, took the only available space—on the open deck. The space below was packed with wounded German soldiers A sister ship, also loaded with Estonian refugees, sank with only one survivor, and the Auliks' vessel encountered storms, but made it to a German-occupied port in Poland, on the Eastern Baltic.

Hearing the news, Paula's mother feared her family had been aboard the doomed boat. She was overjoyed when she heard that they had instead arrived safely. Soon, however, the Soviets, aiming to collectivize agriculture, seized her farm and stripped it of livestock, crops and seeds. Her husband had died. Stranded and alone, she starved to death.

In Poland, German soldiers herded the Estonians into a warehouse and ordered them to strip. Circumcised men and boys were identified as Jews, packed into cattle cars, and sent to death

Come Back Moo

camps. *A rabbi was initially overlooked. The next day he was beaten and sent away. Paula, her four children, her sister and the other surviving Estonians were deloused with DDT while their clothes were heated in an oven to kill lice. They were then packed into cattle cars and sent to a German slave-labor camp on the Elbe River, where Paula was conscripted for daily farm labor. Jews were housed in a separate dormitory and slaved at factories producing the V-2 rocket. One morning the Estonians woke up to find the Jews gone, almost surely to death camps.*

Food was scarce. Farmers paid Paula with potatoes—not enough for her family. The refugees scrounged for anything edible. Paula one day found a can of pure lard—a rare treat for the Auliks. Illness swept the camp. Jaak, the toddler, got so sick he almost died, and Arvo survived sieges of diphtheria and typhoid.

Back on his feet, he became a vital procurer of food for the family. American and British air forces frequently bombed the area. The refugees huddled in pitch-dark bomb shelters. When they came out, Arvo and other boys dived into the river for fish that had been killed or stunned by errant bombs. Stray munitions were lying around, and Arvo stunned more fish by throwing hand grenades into the river. He also sneaked into nearby rail yards and filched foods intended for German troops. He was seven or eight years old.

When the war finally ended in May 1945, the Auliks were on their own, but in the Russian zone of Germany. For three months, they headed west with a band of Estonian refugees, on foot, by oxcart, occasionally by hopping a train, desperate to reach the American zone. They were so hungry they sometimes ate grass.

When they approached the border, the Russians stopped them. The border scene was fluid and chaotic. American soldiers, observing the plight of the young Aulik family and other refugees, picked up the border signs one night and carried them, literally, over the heads of the refugees, expanding the American zone to include Paula, her children and her sister, Vaike.

They were safe, but they were stuck in a displaced persons camp, and there they stayed for four years. Vaike married a fellow Estonian. In 1947 Paula gave birth to a fifth child, Tiina, whose father, also a refugee, brought food to the family and treated the children well.

The United States accepted only refugees in good health, with a real job awaiting them, or under the sponsorship of a religious organization. The U.S. rejected Vaike because she had been exposed to tuberculosis. She and her husband were accepted by Australia, and emigrated there. In 1949 Paula and her five children earned sponsorship by the Lutheran World Federation.

Come Back Moo

The Aulik family shortly after arriving in the United States. Front row, left to right, Arvo, Paula, Tiina and Inge. Back row, Jaak and Helju.

The Auliks landed in the U.S. March 11, 1949, aboard the Ernie Pyle, an army transport ship. Paula was thirty-five, Helju fifteen, Inge fourteen, Arvo twelve, Jaak eight, Tiina twenty-one months. Their employment was in Nebraska. Arvo celebrated his thirteenth birthday as a farm laborer. Paula went to work as laundress in a hospital in Holdredge, Nebraska, carrying Tiina to work with her. She wasn't paid much. The family lived in a small basement apartment. Arvo joined them when time came for school. The Aulik children learned English quickly, excelled in their studies, and worked—as many as three part-time jobs at a time for

Arvo, starting with milk delivery at 3am. Paula got a better job, in charge of food services at a new hospital in Holdredge.

Arvo, 13, with Evelyn and Bill Zimmerman, who employed the newly-arrived refugee to work on their Nebraska farm. When Paula visited and saw how thin he had become, she took him home to the family's basement apartment in Holdredge, Nebraska. He soon was delivering milk at 3 am.

Then their lives began to change. Helju got the summer job at Fair Hills Resort, and met Moo and Maw. At a Sunday service, they heard her describe her wartime experiences and were electrified. Paula got cervical cancer and underwent surgery, so Helju left Fair Hills to care for her mother. She opened her mail one day and found a check from Moo covering her entire tuition for the next year of graduate school at the University of Kansas.

Jaak, the handsome little brother, excelled in high school sports, raising the esteem and reputation of this poor but accomplished refugee family. Moo and Maw helped him, too. All five Aulik children earned college degrees, married, and went on to successful careers. With a PhD in history, Helju enjoyed a distinguished career as a professor at New York University in Buffalo. Jaak served as a Marine captain in Vietnam, then climbed the executive ranks at AT&T. Tiina was a medical technician. (Inge died in 2005.)

Arvo rose to an executive position at Union Electric Company (now AmerenUE) in St. Louis. Shortly after Arvo and his wife, Suzanne, moved to St. Louis, Paula visited them and introduced herself to Moo and Maw so she could thank them for paying Helju's tuition. Moo and Maw welcomed Paula, and loved being a part, however small, of her accomplished life. Paula began visiting twice a year, bringing her youngest child, Tiina. Moo and Maw were in their 80's. They still spent summers at Fair Hills, still helped pay tuition for deserving young women. But Paula, Helju and the Auliks were at the top of their list.

So, too, were their great-grandchildren, the two sons and one daughter of my wife, Jenny, and me. As a gift of survival into their 90's, Moo and Maw knew them well, and they had the good fortune to spend time with two very special great-grandparents. They saw Chris, our eldest, take his first steps.

Moo and Maw celebrating their fiftieth wedding anniversary, September ninth, 1953.

The whole family still congregated at Fair Hills every summer. Moo and Maw flew up. Alden, a college professor with a flexible summer schedule, drove their car up so they would have it for trips to town while being spared the three-day highway trip. Mom and Dad came for five weeks.

Come Back Moo

In 1967, the St. Louis Cardinals won another pennant. I badly wanted to take the family to the World Series, as Moo had done for Alden and me a quarter of a century before. But tickets were scarce. Anheuser-Busch owned the team, and Gussie Busch, the CEO, gave most of the tickets that normally would be available to Cardinal fans to his Budweiser distributors

Luckily, I had an inside track. Jenny, our three children and I were living in Detroit, where I was the bureau manager for United Press International (UPI), then a prominent international news service. Each major league team was allowed to buy a generous ration of World Series tickets. Through my job, I knew the Detroit Tigers' general manager, Jim Campbell, and his public relations manager, Hal Middlesworth. The Tigers had lost the American League pennant race to the Boston Red Sox on the final day of the season—I covered the game—and I suspected the Tiger brass wouldn't use all their tickets for World Series games in St. Louis.

So I asked if I could buy eight tickets from the Tigers for each of the three games in St. Louis. Sure, they said. So our family, four generations, watched the Cardinals beat the Red Sox for the World Championship. (*Bob Gibson pitched and won three games!*) We ranged in age from our sons Andy, six, and Chris, eight, to Moo, eighty-six. Walking from our car to Busch Stadium, we ran into

Campbell, Middlesworth and other Tiger executives, to whom I proudly introduced Moo and the rest of our family.

Back in suburban St. Louis, Dad—our stepfather, Bob Burkitt—bought a house in a new development of modern single-story houses, and persuaded Moo and Maw to buy next door. He and Moo played chess regularly, and Moo and Maw moved into Mother and Dad's social group as their own contemporaries died. Finally, in his eighties, Moo began to enjoy a drink—one, preferably a daiquiri, which he would toss down in a gulp. *Refill, Mr. Bowmar? Nope.* And this at cocktail parties only, which were frequent at Fair Hills, where Moo and Maw were lionized. (Maw stayed on the wagon.) If Fair Hills had been a town with elected officials, Moo would have been mayor: landslide vote.

His dignity was compromised just once. Standing and stretching to open the window by their dining room table, his pants fell down to his ankles, exposing his white legs and his one-piece underwear. Mother made great conversational fun of this, but Moo did not like the subject to be raised and did not laugh or even smile when it was.

Maw's health began to fail. At Fair Hills, Moo supported her as they walked across the footbridge and up the slight incline to the dining room. She no longer walked with him on the golf course, and at age eighty-eight, she and Moo stopped making the trip, after thirty-some years. She fell at home, suffered a broken hip, recovered, but lost strength and stamina. On June 4, 1970, Maw suffered a heart attack and a small stroke. She came home, but five days later she fell in the living room.

She steadily weakened. On June fourteenth Alden and I flew to St. Louis. Mother served lunch and dinner, Maw (according to Moo's diary) glorying in sharing the table with her grandsons. I stayed at the Bowmar house. Moo and I carried Maw to the bathroom during the night and lifted her into a chair for breakfast and lunch. At 1:30pm on June 16, 1970, an ambulance took Maw to a nursing home, with the family following.

I visited the next morning. Maw was distraught. The staff had been told to provide the breakfast she was accustomed to eating every day—whole wheat toast, bacon, fruit (no more Ralston)—but they brought her pancakes instead. Her mind was wandering. She said she feared an electrical explosion,

Within a few days, she was dead, at ninety. Moo was eighty-eight. He came to Fair Hills alone that summer and we joined him there for two weeks, Mother and Dad for five weeks, as was the family custom. But he didn't have the same prime lakeside cabin, and he didn't have his wife. They had been married sixty-seven years.

William B. Mead

On May 16, 1971, Paula and Tiina, Paula's youngest child, arrived in St. Louis for five days, and were entertained daily by Moo, Mother and Dad and their friends. Moo had a wonderful time. He had booked a cruise starting June first, accompanied by Frances Inglis, a platonic friend, widow of the First Congregational Church's longtime minister and Bowmar friend. But first he wanted to take care of something important.

His diary had to catch up: "Probably 5/27 Thursday or Fri. 5/28 engaged to Paula by phone." He was eighty-nine, had been a widower for a lonesome year, and offered her the remainder of his life with two conditions: She had to learn to drive and to play bridge. Paula agreed, with the approval of her children. But nothing interrupted Moo's schedule, so on June first he flew to New York, spent that night at the Commodore Hotel, where he always stayed—room $25, or $133 in 2010 dollars-- and boarded his cruise ship the next day with Mrs. Inglis. When Missouri night was held onboard twelve women and one man showed up. Moo was elected State Representative.

Seas were rough, with one or two port stops cancelled and many of the passengers under the weather, but Moo never got seasick. He didn't miss a meal, a bridge game or a shore excursion. He wrote to everyone, Paula repeatedly, and he bought her "a very lovely bag."

Moo still had a full head of white hair. He looked much younger than his years, and he liked to needle old men he met, asking them their ages. "Eighty? Why, you're still a kid!" he would exult, boasting of his own advanced age.

Moo took Paula to Versailles, Kentucky, that October to meet the Bowmar and Fishback clans. One dear relative, a somewhat dotty woman of middle age, was notorious for always being late—sometimes by hours—even to tightly scheduled family events. Moo told her he would pick her up at an appointed hour, and if she wasn't ready to walk out the door, purse in hand, he would go on without her. He did it once, and she learned to be ready.

Moo's ninetieth birthday was approaching. At Fair Hills, Wave Hays, an old Ralston Purina colleague, and his wife, Ginny, threw a ninetieth birthday party. Lots of summer vacation friends turned out. Moo downed his one daiquiri, got expansive, and disclosed his plan to marry Paula.

Two days before Moo's ninetieth birthday, back home, we threw him a celebratory luncheon at Algonquin Country Club. All the family friends were there, including the Auliks, who sat together at one of the dozen or so tables. Moo, Mother, Dad, Alden and I presided at a head table, and we all toasted Moo, and roasted him a little. He was last on the agenda, and after gracefully delivering thanks and witticisms, he said, "And tomorrow, at the Congregational Church, Paula Aulik and I will be married." He gestured to his fiancée.

The crowd was bowled over. Some thought Moo was joking, and to some extent he was, explaining that he'd be ninety in two days and thought that was too old to get married, so he'd beat it by a day. Those who caught on applauded heartily. Others were still scratching their heads as they left. Mother, Dad, Alden and I knew it was coming, but nevertheless we were thrilled. Yes, we told incredulous friends, it was true.

Head table at dinner honoring Moo two days before his ninetieth birthday in 1971. Left to right, our daughter—Moo's great-granddaughter—Meagan; Mother; Moo; Jenny, my wife and Moo's granddaughter-in-law; me, Bill

Come Back Moo

Mead, standing; and brother Alden. Our sons Chris and Andy were also there.

For at least two years, Moo had been mailing Paula a monthly check to augment her small earnings. She brought all that money to the wedding, presenting it as her dowry—this poor woman had saved every penny of Moo's gifts. Moo wept.

William B. Mead

Come Back Moo

Moo, one day short of ninety years old, cutting his wedding cake with Paula, his new bride. She was 57. Mother—Moo's daughter—is at far left. Her husband, Bob Burkitt, is at far right.

Paula took bridge lessons and driving lessons—duck soup for a woman who had survived and achieved so much more. She settled smoothly into the role of prosperous suburban housewife. She cooked, gardened and entertained. Ruth Sleet was still preparing three meals a day, though Paula would have preferred to do that herself.

William B. Mead

Mother and Dad had a television set, as did most American families, but Moo scorned the new medium. He read as much as ever although he needed a magnifying glass as well as strong reading glasses. Paula finally let it be known that she might enjoy watching an occasional TV show; maybe just the news. Moo ordered one and had it set up out of the way, with one armchair. Paula, a very sensitive and considerate wife, didn't watch often.

Moo swept Paula into his social and traveling life, happily presenting his younger wife to fellow cruise passengers. I happened to be in New York as they were embarking on an Atlantic crossing, and I got aboard to see them off. Jaak Aulik also was there. Moo was in his element, smiling and joking, showing us around the ship.

Their next cruise—as usual, aboard a Swedish cruise ship, Moo's favorite line—was on the Pacific. It was the fall of 1973. Moo took sick. Paula took him to the ship's doctor, whose diagnosis was not encouraging—kidney failure. Alden, a distinguished chemistry professor at the University of Minnesota, enlisted a colleague to handle his classes and flew to Sydney, Australia, to meet the ship. He saw Paula on the deck and caught her attention. "He's holding his own," she shouted.

Come Back Moo

But not for long. Moo was hospitalized, bedridden. Paula sat beside him all day, every day. Moo slept much of the time, but conversed when up to it. In the hotel, Alden remembers seeing Moo's hat, and wondering whether he would ever wear it again. After a week, Moo began to improve. His doctors were optimistic. Alden flew back to Minneapolis.

But Moo's condition worsened, and his mind wandered. Paula held his hand. She could tell he was near death. "Let me go now," he told her. "It will be all right." He died, and I flew to Sydney to bring Paula home. Her sister, Vaike, joined us for a brief service at a crematorium. Paula and I checked out of the hotel and went to the airport. It was a very long trip, flying from Sydney to Honolulu to Los Angeles to St. Louis. All the way, Paula held the urn containing Moo's ashes. I slept, for the first time since leaving home in Maryland more than a day before.

The flight landed in St. Louis at three am. Arvo, Paula's son, and his wife, Suzanne, were there to meet us. Paula still held the urn with Moo's ashes. She would not let it go.

It is 1940. I'm six. Alden is seven. We've finished dinner and MyMy, the maid, is washing the dishes. Maw has settled into her rocking chair, playing solitaire on a big board on her lap. Mother is reading. We follow Moo to the sunroom and sit side-by-side on the big armchair. Moo sits in his rocker and, with relish, starts reading aloud. It's Robinson Crusoe, by Daniel Defoe. The hero is marooned. How will he survive?

So many years ago. Come back. Please. Come back, Moo.

Thank you for reading.

Please review this book. Reviews help others find Absolutely Amazing eBooks and inspire us to keep providing these marvelous tales.

If you would like to be put on our email list to receive updates on new releases, contests, and promotions, please go to AbsolutelyAmazingEbooks.com and sign up.

About the Author

William B. Mead, a former UPI bureau chief and Washington correspondent, is the author of six books on baseball history. He and his wife live in Bethesda, Maryland.

The New Atlantian Library

NewAtlantianLibrary.com
or AbsolutelyAmazingEbooks.com
or AA-eBooks.com

www.ingramcontent.com/pod-product-compliance
Lightning Source LLC
Chambersburg PA
CBHW050837160426
43192CB00011B/2065